BEST OF

TRY THIS ONE

The most **popular** ideas from
the **#1 youth ministry resource**

foreword
Thom Schultz

Group resources actually work!

This Group resource helps you focus on **"The 1 Thing®"**—a life-changing relationship with Jesus Christ. "The 1 Thing" incorporates our **R.E.A.L.** approach to ministry. It reinforces a growing friendship with Jesus, encourages long-term learning, and results in life transformation, because it's:

Relational
Learner-to-learner interaction enhances learning and builds Christian friendships.

Experiential
What learners experience through discussion and action sticks with them up to 9 times longer than what they simply hear or read.

Applicable
The aim of Christian education is to equip learners to be both hearers and doers of God's Word.

Learner-based
Learners understand and retain more when the learning process takes into consideration how they learn best.

Best of Try This One From Group Magazine
The Most Popular Ideas From the #1 Youth Ministry Resource

Visit our Web site: **www.group.com**

Credits
Contributors: Hundreds of youth workers
Editor: E. Paul Allen
Creative Development Editor: Dave Thornton
Chief Creative Officer: Joani Schultz
Designer: Veronica Lucas
Print Production Artist: Julia Martin
Cover Art Director: Jeff Storm
Cover Designer: Jeff Storm
Production Manager: DeAnne Lear

Unless otherwise indicated, all Scripture quotations are taken from the *Holy Bible*, New Living Translation, copyright © 1996, 2004. Used by permission of Tyndale House Publishers, Inc., Wheaton, Illinois 60189. All rights reserved.

Library of Congress Cataloging-in-Publication Data
Best of try this one from Group magazine : the most popular ideas from the #1 youth ministry resource. -- 1st American pbk. ed.
    p. cm.
  Includes index.
  ISBN-13: 978-0-7644-3414-3 (pbk. : alk. paper)
  1. Church work with teenagers. 2. Church work with youth. I. Group Publishing.
  BV4447.B49 2006
  268'.433--dc22

                    2006028634

10 9 8 7 6 5 4 3 2 1   15 14 13 12 11 10 09 08 07 06
Printed in the United States of America.

FOREWORD BY THOM SCHULTZ
INTRODUCTION

This stuff works. The ideas in this book come from people like you—in the thick of youth ministry.

Here you'll find a motherlode of practical youth ministry ideas for Bible studies, outreach programs, devotions, games, crowdbreakers, discussion starters, and attention-grabbers. They were all developed in the field and sent to Group Magazine's highly popular "Try This One" department.

When I started Group in 1974, there was no World Wide Web—no electronic networking for youth workers or anyone else. But there was definitely a need to share good ideas among those "in the trenches." That was the dream for Group Magazine. And the section called "Try This One" quickly became a real favorite among readers who looked forward to the usefulness, fun, and authenticity of reader-submitted ideas. In those pre-www days, "Try This One" was a low-tech offline forum.

And "Try This One" continues to be a favorite in Group, which is the most-read youth ministry resource in the world. Some things just work and keep on working. God has certainly blessed many youth ministries through the shared ideas in "Try This One."

In this book, we've collected the best "Try This One" ideas that have been submitted in recent years. So dig in, enjoy, and use these ideas in your ministry. They work! And join the long tradition of sharing the best youth ministry ideas. Send your great ideas to Group Magazine at editor@groupmag.com. Who knows—maybe your idea will make it into the magazine and the next edition of this book.

Thom Schultz

Every youth leader comes to that moment in ministry when he or she confronts the age-old question: *What are we gonna do for this?* That's why we decided over two decades ago to introduce "Try This One," proven ideas that you, the practitioner, have used in your student ministry.

The very first book published by Group was a collection of the best of "Try This One" from Group magazine. We haven't done another book like it for decades and felt like it was time. So, we opened up the "Try This One" vault and gathered the best ideas we could to create another book for you. As we started going through ideas, we were reminded again of the great things you're doing to build relationships with the teenagers.

This book is a collection of those ideas, provided in easy-to-follow sections that will allow you to browse through and plan for the future or pick up the book on the run and pull out an idea you can use today. We encourage you to make this book a daily ministry tool. Mark it up, write the date over each idea you use, rate each idea according to its impact in your group, and pass it on to your lay leaders.

For your convenience, the sections are divided as follows: Bible Studies, Crowdbreakers, Discussion Starters, Fund-Raisers, Games, Group Builders, Helpful Hints, and Outreach. Each idea summarizes everything you need for the activity, and the different sections make it easy to find exactly what you need.

We're always looking for fresh and effective ministry ideas, so send us your "Try This One" idea. If we use your idea, we'll pay you $50. Just send your idea, daytime phone number, and a self-addressed, stamped envelope to Group's "Try This One," P. O. Box 481, Loveland, Colorado 80538-0481 or e-mail editor@groupmag.com.

Enjoy trying the best ideas out there!

TRY THIS ONE

1. PROVERB CAPTIONS

Five minutes into this Bible study on Proverbs, the giggling begins!

For this Bible study, you'll need a stack of the tackiest supermarket tabloids you can find. You'll also need paper, glue, and a few mainstream magazines, such as Time or Newsweek.

Distribute the tabloids. Explain that much of the Bible talks about planning for the coming kingdom and leading a prayerful life, but the book of Proverbs was written to get us through this life, here and now, one day at a time. Pass out Bibles, and tell your kids to use any verse they want from the book of Proverbs as a caption for a picture from the tabloids. Have kids write the verses on paper and glue the pictures on the paper.

Chuckles and giggles will soon lead to laughing out loud! Then pull out the mainstream magazines or newspapers, and tell the group to find captions, once again, from Proverbs. Have them glue these pictures and captions onto different pieces of paper. This time, the captions will be more relevant. Hang the pictures in the hallway of your church so congregation members will see them. Close with a prayer, asking God to make these Scriptures apply to your teenagers' lives today.

Steve Case
Oviedo, Florida

2. BIGGER AND BETTER

This study helps kids understand the value of God's blessings.

Begin the Bible study with a Bigger and Better scavenger hunt. Divide your group into teams of four or five, and give each group a can of soup. Tell them they have 15 minutes to trade their cans of soup with someone who will give them something bigger and better. If your meeting place doesn't easily warrant kids trading with others, give the can of soup to one person in each group, and ask him or her to try and trade with other members of the group. After 15 minutes, compare the trades and declare one the "biggest and best" trade.

Then ask each group to read Genesis 25:29-34, and discuss the following questions:

- How hard was it to trade your can of soup?
- How hard was it for Esau to trade his birthright for soup?
- Do you think Esau ever regretted his decision? Why or why not?
- What are some of God's blessings that teenagers might trade for something they think will bring them happiness?
- Why would they give up these blessings?
- Do you think teenagers will regret giving up these things?
- How can God help you know what to trade and what to keep?

Close with a popcorn prayer, asking each person to name one thing he or she will hold onto and offer to God for use in his kingdom.

Lisa Nichols Hickman
Tucson, Arizona

3. ONE BODY, MANY PARTS

Use 1 Corinthians 12:12-31 to spark a discussion on how individual talent can contribute to the body of Christ.

For this activity, you'll first need to create a sculpture from various items. For example, you might use LEGO construction toys, modeling clay, wood, paper, PVC pipe, coat hangers, cardboard, paints, boxes, or sheets of plastic. Then place the sculpture out of sight, and set out a selection of the same items you used to build the sculpture. Separate your class into groups of four, and assign each group member one of the following body parts: Eyes, Ears, Feet, or Hands. Then have all the Eyes from each group gather together in one area, have the Ears gather in another area, and so on. Use the following rules to have groups create sculptures similar to your sculpture:

(1) The Eyes are the only ones who can see the sculpture.

(2) The Eyes describe to the Ears what they saw.

(3) The Ears tell the Feet what they heard.

(4) The Feet gather the materials needed and tell the Hands what they heard.

(5) The Hands create the sculpture according to the information they receive.

Continue passing information this way through many rounds, until the sculptures are complete. When groups have finished their sculptures, reveal your original sculpture and discuss these questions:

• How is your sculpture different from everyone else's?

• Would you have made the same sculpture if you didn't have the Ear in your group? the Eye?

Then read aloud 1 Corinthians 12:12-31 in the following manner: Everyone reads verses 12-14; Feet read verse 15; Ears read verse 16; Eyes read verse 17; everyone reads verses 18-20; Hands read verse 21; and you read verses 22-31. Afterward, have the groups discuss these questions:

• Why did the Apostle Paul choose the human body to illustrate everyone's role in the church?

• How can you rely on others in the church?

• How can the church rely on you?

• What part of the body of Christ are you?

Close in prayer, asking God to help guide each person in determining his or her part in the body of Christ.

Tammy Weissling
Thief River Falls, Minnesota

TRY THIS ONE

4. WARNING LABEL

Use silly warning labels to inspire teenagers to reflect on their commitment to Christ.

Do an Internet search for "silly warning labels" to find silly but actual warning labels. Create a list and distribute the lists to your students. Then have a chuckle about how silly it is that people need to be warned about these things. Ask:

• Why do you think these products have these silly warning labels?

• If you had to wear a warning label, what might it be?

Have groups of three or four read the following passages together: Luke 9:23-27; 9:57-62; and 18:18-30. Ask:

• In these verses, what does Jesus say we might have to give up for him?

• When people decide to follow Jesus, why might they not think about what it may cost them?

• Have you been surprised by something that you've had to sacrifice because of your commitment to Christ?

Give students each a sheet of paper and ask:

• If Christianity had a warning label, what might it be?

Then have each student draw a cross on the paper and add a warning label.

John Pape
Rising Sun, Indiana

5. RULES AND AUTHORITY—SO WHAT!

Use a game without rules to help young people understand why rules are important.

Have kids form groups of four to six, and give each group a board game to play. Tell everyone that the rules of the games are as follows: There are no rules, and no one is in charge! After about 10 minutes, have groups discuss these questions.

• How does the game change when there are no rules?

• Why do you think there are rules?

• What are some rules that protect us?

• Do you obey those rules?

• What do you do when you don't like a certain rule?

Say: Often rules don't make sense to us. And sometimes the authorities will let us down. We end up confused or frustrated, just as we did with these games. But God didn't plan things that way. He uses rules to protect us. When God sets the rules, he will never let us down.

Read aloud Romans 13:1-7. Then have groups discuss these questions:

• Does this Scripture change the way you think about rules and authority? Why or why not?

• What are some situations where you struggle with authority?

• How can we help each other with these struggles? How can God help us?

Close in prayer, asking kids to pray for specific people in authority, for a healthy attitude toward these people, and for each person's struggles with authority.

Tammy Bovee
Burton, Michigan

6. BRICK PROMISES

Use bricks to illustrate that holding on to our burdens can build barriers between us and God.

Ask:

- What are some things that typically create anxiety for people?
- What methods do people use to cope with anxiety?

Have students form pairs or trios, and read 1 Peter 5:7 and Psalm 55:22. Ask:

- Have you experienced offering your stress to God, only to continue having that stress afterward? Explain.
- Why are we so often unable to completely give our worries over to God in spite of God's promises?
- What specific steps can help us?

Then cart a wheelbarrow of bricks into your meeting room. You'll need one brick for each student. Have each person take a brick and use a permanent marker to write a word or draw a picture that describes or symbolizes something that's causing stress. Then have students begin building a low brick wall with their bricks. After the wall is finished, ask:

- How do these burdens form a barrier between God and us?
- How does God use our burdens to bring us closer to him?

Then ask students to remove their bricks and write on the back: "I will give it to God." Have students find partners and pray together, asking God to help them release their burdens. Tell students to take their bricks home with them as a reminder to give all their worries daily—and completely—on God.

Paul Baldwin
Mishawaka, Indiana

7. SERVING OTHERS, SERVING GOD

Prep your group for a service project or a missions trip with a study based on John 13.

You'll need a sheet, tape, acrylic paint, soapy water, clean water, towels, a CD with Third Day's song "City on a Hill," and a CD player.

Before your next missions trip, paint the name, date, and location of your project at the top of a large sheet and attach it to the wall of your meeting room. Set out the paint and tubs of water. Read aloud John 13:1-5, 12-17. Ask a volunteer to dip a hand in paint and leave a handprint on the sheet. Then wash the volunteer's hand, and have that person wash the next person's hand after he or she leaves a handprint. Continue until the last person washes your hand after you leave a handprint. Then ask:

- How did it feel to have someone wash your hand? to wash someone else's hand?
- How is leaving your handprint like your role on our trip?

Have trios read the following verses: Psalm 123:1; Matthew 25:40; Colossians 3:23. Ask:

- How does the work you do with your hands reflect God's love?
- How do you serve God as you serve others?
- What do you hope to give—and receive—on this mission trip?

Close by playing the song "City on a Hill" and praying together silently.

Denise Prange
High Ridge, Missouri

8. REVOLUTIONARY WATER BALLOON WAR

Introduce kids to a round of "trench warfare," and launch a study on spiritual warfare.

Form two teams, and give each team a stock of water balloons. Have teams line up facing each other, about 15 to 20 feet apart.

Choose a team to go first, then allow everyone on that team to throw water balloons at the other team—all at the same time. If someone is hit, he or she must sit out. Then allow the second team to throw water balloons. Have three rounds of balloon throwing for each team. Whichever team has the most people standing after three rounds wins. Explain that this balloon battle is similar to how battles were fought in the Revolutionary War. Ask:

- Was one team stronger than the other?
- How were you feeling when the other team had a chance to throw? Explain.
- What helped you unite in battle?

Read aloud 2 Corinthians 10:3-5. Then ask:

- What does Paul mean when he says, "We do not wage a war as the world does"?
- How much importance do you give to the idea of spiritual warfare, and why?
- What kinds of enemies do we fight against?
- What weapon do you rely on most in waging spiritual warfare?
- What's one additional weapon you can add to your arsenal?
- What are some specific ways we can support each other in this battle?

T.J. Roberts
Salt Lake City, Utah

9. BIBLE SURVIVOR

Use outcast characters from the Bible in a Survivor-type game to teach about Christ's unconditional love.

For this Bible study, you'll need to create a player profile for each person in your group. Use the Bible to find people who could've been considered outcasts, such as a leper, tax collector, blind person, crippled person, shepherd, Roman centurion, fisherman, prophet, or demon-possessed person. Write a short profile for each that explains why that person might be an outcast. Give each teenager a profile.

Have kids sit in a circle and, in character, tell everyone else who they are. Then have each person write on a piece of paper the character he or she wants to vote out of the game, based on who contributes the least to society. Between rounds of voting, allow the "survivors" to give a short reason why they should be allowed to stay in the group. When four people remain, allow the "outcasts" to vote for the final survivor.

After the game, read aloud Matthew 5:1-12. Then discuss the following questions:

- How do you think Jesus would view our "outcasts"?
- How would you describe unconditional love?
- How important to you or your friends is someone's appearance or social status?
- How is the way others see us different from the way God sees us?

Jeff Browning and Chris Coletti
Vista, California

10. LESSONS FROM THE DRIVE-THROUGH

Turn a fast-food experience into a teachable moment for your youth group members.

To begin a Sunday morning Bible study, take your group out for breakfast. Go to a fast-food restaurant with a drive-through window. After you've picked up your order, take your group to a comfortable place to eat breakfast as you study Scripture. Start by asking kids to talk about what happens at the drive-through that could describe their walks of faith. (For example, you may have to wait or what you want is not on the menu.)

Then discuss the following questions, using corresponding Scripture to answer each question:

- Why is "waiting" an important part of your faith walk? (Psalm 25:5; 27:14; 40:1-3; Isaiah 30:18; and Philippians 3:20)

- What do you do when what you want "isn't on the menu"? How do you resist or accept God's plan? (Jeremiah 29:11)

- How do you know what God is trying to tell you? How do you communicate with God? How does God communicate with you? (2 Chronicles 7:14; Jeremiah 33:3; and 1 Corinthians 2:9-10)

- What "exchanges" take place in your walk of faith? What are you giving to God? What did Christ pay for, and what did you get in return? (James 2:18 and 1 John 2:2)

Chrisann Goad
Arlington, Texas

11. LASER BIBLE

Don't let your next laser tag outing go by without adding a teachable moment!

You'll need Bibles with concordances, paper, and pens or pencils.

Form small groups, and have each group list words related to laser tag. For example, "fast-paced," "fear," "mission," "darkness," "hide," or "teams." Ask groups to choose one word from their list that might also relate to the Christian life. Have groups look up that word in a concordance and write the Scripture references next to their chosen word. Then have each group member look up one of the listed Scripture references and write a few thoughts on how the laser tag word also relates to his or her faith.

Your group might come up with ideas like these:

- Darkness (Psalm 18:28)—God is with us in good times (light) as well as bad (dark).
- Fear (Psalm 27:1)—When we remember the salvation God promises, we don't need to be afraid.
- Hide (Matthew 5:14-16)—We should never hide our faith from the world.

After teams have shared their ideas, discuss these questions:

- How is a game of laser tag like your walk of faith?
- Which of the Scriptures we read is the most encouraging to you? Explain.
- How can you use the Bible as your "weapon" against sin and evil?

Debra Brauner
Pottstown, Pennsylvania

12. SEEK AND YE SHALL FIND

(Especially effective with junior highers)

This fast-paced mall activity is a fun Bible study that puts a twist on the game Where's Waldo?

Form teams of two to four young people. Then assign six adult volunteers each a distinct feature that teams will identify. Ask each adult to choose a favorite Bible verse to give to the young people. You might use the following suggestions for "distinct features":

1. Person sitting on a phone book (Psalm 105:1-2)

2. Person with a dime taped under his or her shoe (1 Timothy 6:6-10)

3. Person with a black walking cast (Isaiah 35:3-6)

4. Person with glasses (Hebrews 11:1)

5. Person wearing zipper pants with the bottom portion of one leg missing (Proverbs 4:11-12)

6. Person wearing the bottom portion of a zipper pants leg on his or her head (1 Corinthians 1:27-28)

Ask your volunteers to scatter throughout the mall (not inside stores) and change locations after any team finds them. When a team finds an adult, the adult will tell the team his or her verse.

Ask two more adults to act as Timers, who send each team on a mission by saying (for example), "Seek and ye shall find...a person sitting on a phone book. Bring me back the good news." The teams, with Bibles, will go find that adult. Make sure that teams know not to go inside stores. They can introduce themselves and their church's name to any person who might be sitting, saying that they are on a "seek and find" mission and asking the person if her or she is sitting on a phone book. After the teams find the adult, they run back and read the Bible verse to the Timers before receiving their next mission. The Timers will then send teams off to look for another adult.

End the game after a certain amount of time or when one team has accomplished all six missions. Arrange with the adults to meet the teams at the food court afterward for snacks and Bible verse discussion. Ask:

• How is this activity like your faith journey?

• Which Bible verse meant the most to you and why?

• Does the verse you chose challenge you to change in any way? Explain.

We had so much fun that several other teenagers who'd stopped to watch ended up joining the game!

Angela Breidenbach
Missoula, Montana

13. SHOPPING-BAG SERMONS

This is a great way to get kids to dig into their Bibles and use their creativity.

Have the youth group form teams of four to six people. Give each team a shopping bag containing three to four random items, such as old keys, spoons, action figures, hockey pucks, lipstick, staplers, or unusual vegetables. The stranger the items, the better! Tell teams they have 15 to 20 minutes to come up with a sermon based on the items in the bag. The rules are:

    (1) The sermon must have three points, each based on the items in their bags;

    (2) The sermon has to be at least three minutes long;

    (3) The sermon must include Scripture;

    (4) The sermon must include one creative element such as a drama, song, or poem; and

    (5) Everyone on the team has to be involved.

The sermons that our kids came up with were hilarious, creative, and very insightful…we had a blast!

Dan Bursey
Lewisporte, Newfoundland

14. THE JESUS IN ME

This Bible study will help your teenagers reflect and understand what it means to have an identity through Jesus.

You'll need Bibles, newsprint, markers, scissors, and tape.

Trace the outline of one teenager onto newsprint, cut it out, and tape it to a wall. Tell young people to list words on the cutout that describe the typical appearance, attitudes, and actions of a teenager.

Then tell kids to list on the cutout the spiritual characteristics a teenager would have when he or she is in a relationship with Jesus. Have kids discuss these questions:

• Why is it more difficult to describe spiritual characteristics?

• What are some words you think God would use to describe a teenager?

Form groups of three or four. Have each group trace another outline of someone in the group and cut it out. Assign each group one of the following passages: Ephesians 1:1-12; 1:13-23; 2:4-10; and 2:19-22. Have the groups write the Scripture references at the tops of their cutouts.

Say: Read aloud your passage, and listen carefully for the characteristics of those who have a relationship with Jesus. Decorate your cutout with pictures and words that symbolize the characteristics reflected in the passage. When everyone is finished, ask groups to explain their cutouts and what they drew or wrote on them. Then have them tape their cutouts to a wall. Ask:

• Why is it important to know who we are spiritually?

• How might seeing yourself through Jesus influence the way you act or think?

Have a volunteer read aloud Romans 12:5-21. Ask:

• What does "good works" mean?

• What does it mean to be saved by grace—not by works?

Say: There are many ways to describe who we are in Jesus. These cutouts are reminders of how we are each a special creation made by God, who has claimed us and our characteristics—both typical and spiritual.

Peter and Karen Theodore
Dumfries, Virginia

TRY THIS ONE

15. THE FACE OF JESUS

Use this lesson to get young people to think about Jesus and to explore Scripture for ideas about what he might really have looked like.

Before the meeting collect a dozen or more pictures of Jesus. Be sure to include some that depict him as white, blue-eyed, and cleanly groomed. You can find tons of images on the Internet. For example, go to www.ntgateway.com and click on "Art & Images" for links to a variety of sites. Or visit a search engine, such as Google, and type in "Jesus Christ pictures."

Tape the pictures to the walls of your youth room. After teenagers arrive, have them go around the room to closely observe the images. Then bring them together to discuss what Jesus really looked like. Use this as an opportunity to look into the Bible to discover the real world that Jesus grew up in. Ask:

- Do you think there's anything wrong with these pictures of Jesus? Why or why not?

Say: We don't know what Jesus looked like; there weren't any cameras, no one painted his portrait, and the gospel writers never described his physical appearance. Like you and me, though, Jesus had a face and body that were shaped by his heritage and his life. Let's see what clues we can find in Scripture.

Read aloud Luke 1:26-32. Ask:

- How would Jesus' Jewish heritage have affected his coloring, stature, and overall appearance?

Read aloud Matthew 2:19-23. Ask:

- Jesus grew up in the small town of Nazareth; how would this have affected his manner and appearance?

Read aloud Mark 6:1-4. Ask:

- How would Jesus' years of work as a carpenter have affected him?

Read aloud Isaiah 53:1-3. Say: From the earliest days of Christianity these verses have been interpreted as a reference to Jesus. Ask:

- Are you surprised by this description of him? Why or why not?
- Do you think this refers only to Jesus' disfigurement by his passion, or can you imagine that Jesus' everyday appearance might have been ordinary or even unattractive? Explain.
- If you could look into Jesus' eyes, what do you think you would see there?
- Does your image of Jesus affect the way you relate to him? Why or why not?

Tim Inman
New Brighton, Minnesota

16. GIFTED

Use this study, based on 1 Corinthians 12, to show kids that they each have a unique, God-given role to play as members of the body of Christ.

Have kids form groups of five. Give each group a supply of marshmallows and toothpicks. In another room or somewhere out of sight, have a model constructed out of marshmallows and toothpicks. Each group member has only one role to play. Here's the breakdown:

Player 1—can only use his or her right hand and can only handle toothpicks.

Player 2—can only use his or her left hand and can only handle toothpicks.

Player 3—can only use his or her right hand and can only handle marshmallows.

Player 4—can only use his or her left hand and can only handle marshmallows.

Player 5—This person is the Runner, the only person allowed to see the model and the only person who's allowed to speak. He or she instructs the other group members in constructing a replica of the model. This person isn't allowed to touch anything.

Be sure to enforce all the rules, especially the talking one!

Afterward, have kids answer the following discussion questions:

- Were all the responsibilities equal in this activity, or was one more important than the others? Why or why not?
- Were all the responsibilities in this activity equally hard, or was one harder than the others? Why or why not?

Read aloud 1 Corinthians 12, and then ask:

- What spiritual gifts often seem to us like lesser gifts? Why?
- Why is it often hard to work together with people who have gifts different from our own?
- Why would God insist that it's crucial to honor our differences?
- What's one spiritual gift listed in 1 Corinthians 12 that most reflects one of your spiritual gifts?
- How have you exercised that gift?

Tracy Williams
Springfield, Missouri

TRY THIS ONE

17. FAITH WILL FIND IT!

Use this twist on I Spy to lead teenagers into a Bible study about seeking God.

For this activity, choose a living room or meeting room that has lots of knickknacks, pictures, or decorations. Choose a dozen or more items that can be easily hidden in the room (place a toothpick in the groove of a wooden frame; place a clear marble in the bottom of a glass goblet; attach a matching color of yarn to a lampshade; and so on).

Have teenagers form pairs, and give each pair a checklist of the items. Let kids know that everything's in plain sight but not easily spotted at a glance. Set a time limit, and tell pairs to check off each item as they locate it. When time's up, ask:

- How hard was it to discover the items?
- If you didn't have a checklist, how hard would it have been to find them?

Read aloud Luke 11:9-13. Ask:

- If God wants to be discovered and known, why is the search often difficult?
- What are some items on the "checklist" we can use to search for God?
- In comparison to the effort you exert in other areas of your life, how much energy do you put into seeking God?
- What's one way you've discovered God in your life recently?

Ron Jaworski
Pittsburgh, Pennsylvania

18. THE BIG PICTURE

Most teenagers know many individual Bible stories but have no clue in what order they occurred or how they all fit together. This activity will help them get things straight.

Pick 20 to 40 Bible events, and have teenagers create newspaper headlines for them. For example, a headline for the story of Noah and the ark might read, "100 Percent Chance of Rain—Local Man Builds Boat." The headline for the Tower of Babel story might read, "Construction Halted on Tower—Communication Breaks Down."

Have young people write or type each headline on a different sheet of paper. If you have a desktop publishing program, have kids get creative with different fonts, colors, clip art, and so on. Collect the headlines and form small groups of three. Give each group a few headlines, and then have groups answer these questions:

1. What's the story behind the headline—who are the people and events involved?
2. Where's the story found in the Bible and approximately when did this event occur?
3. What does this Bible event tell us about God and his redemptive plan for his people?
4. If you have time, write a lead paragraph to go along with the headline.

After the groups finish, gather together and have a representative from each group read aloud the group's answers. Then lead a discussion on the chronology of Bible stories.

At the end of your time, post the headline sheets on the wall in order. This is a quick way to help kids get an overall view of the Bible landscape. We did this activity with mostly Old Testament stories—about 35—and covered them in a little more than an hour.

Carl Fuglein
West Chester, Pennsylvania

19. FAITH FOCUS

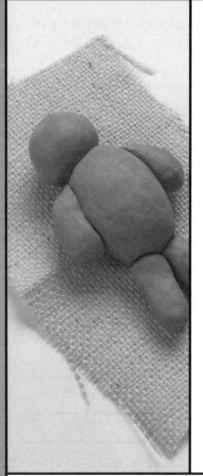

Help your kids understand their faith in God as a concrete thing, not an abstract concept.

You'll need a lump of clay—the kind that dries when it sits out—for each person. (If clay isn't available, use aluminum foil, or have kids find something in the room that represents their faith.)

If you have a large group, break into small groups of no more than seven. Give each person some clay. Say: **You have five minutes to mold your lump of clay into something that represents your faith. It can be anything—abstract or real. For example, a cross could represent Christ dying, or a child could represent a childlike faith.** Encourage a silent and contemplative atmosphere so each person can concentrate.

After five minutes, have people take turns around the circle sharing what they created and how it represents their faith.

Pass out the Bibles, and have volunteers read aloud Hebrews 11. Then ask the following questions:

- What's the hardest part about molding something to represent your faith?
- When you think about your faith, what are you sure of?
- This chapter of Scripture talks about faith being something that we don't necessarily see. How, though, do we sometimes "see" our faith?
- Name several of the things the great men and women of the Bible did by faith. How were they able to do these things? Who was their faith in? Why is the object of one's faith important?
- What are some one-word descriptions of what faith is?

Close in prayer by using single words of thanks and praise. Have kids take their creations home to remind them of their faith, and the object of that faith.

Scott Meier
Norman, Oklahoma

20. SEE, THINK, AND DO

Use this activity to help kids practice the three fundamental disciplines of Bible study: observation, interpretation, and application.

Take your group to a full parking lot—the more crowded the better. Have your group observe a car or a group of cars. Ask them to carefully examine both the car's interior and exterior. Exercise discernment if you decide to study a stranger's car. If necessary, "plant" a church member's car to use as your target vehicle.

After about 10 minutes, gather kids together and ask:

- Based on your observations of this car, what did you learn (interpretation) about its owner?
- What could we do to serve (application) the owner?

Say: For example, you may spot an out-of-state license plate or an infant car seat in a car. The person may be a tourist or have a child. How far away did the owner travel to get where you are? Can you tell the sex of the child? Could the owner of the car use a home-cooked meal if he or she has been on the road a long time? Might the owners need a baby sitter so they can spend an uninterrupted evening together? Ask:

- How are these skills—observation, interpretation, and application—similar to or different from how we read and interpret Scripture?
- How can we use these skills to get more out of our Bible-reading?

Derek Chinn
Portland, Oregon

21. THE REMNANT

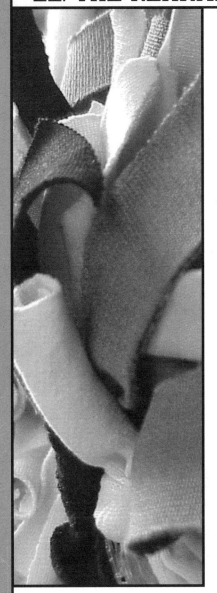

This Bible study works well at a lock-in or retreat.

You'll need a large piece of fabric that will serve as a banner, other remnants of fabric and trim, a large piece of cardboard, pens, scissors, markers, a glue gun, and a dowel. Have each person bring a piece of fabric—a remnant—to the event (big enough to trace a puzzle piece onto).

Draw the shape of a person on the cardboard—the more abstract the better—and cut it out. Trace the outline of the cardboard person onto your banner. Then cut the cardboard person into puzzle pieces— enough so each group member can have one. Make the pieces as different and strange as possible.

At your event, have kids each trace their puzzle piece onto the piece of material they brought, then cut it out. Next, have kids work to put the puzzle together—don't tell them what it is. When they've figured it out, bring out the banner, and have them lay their pieces of material inside the outline. Have someone with good handwriting write "The Remnant" on top of the banner and "Jeremiah 23:3" on the bottom. Ask another volunteer to use a hot glue gun to glue the puzzle pieces to the banner. You can also glue the remnants of trim onto the banner's edges. To hang the banner, glue the dowel on the top of the banner and attach a long piece of trim to hang it.

Next, read aloud Jeremiah 23:1-8. Then ask:

- Who is the remnant mentioned in this Scripture passage?
- How are Christians like or unlike a remnant?
- What is God promising to accomplish and provide for the remnant in these verses?
- What are God's promises to us as Christians today?

Then read aloud Romans 12:4-8 and any other passages discussing the many roles Christians play in the body of Christ. Ask:

- What part do you feel you play in the body of Christ?
- What role do you play in our church?

Close with prayer, thanking God for the gifts represented in your group.

Selena Razey
Franklin, Tennessee

22. SHOE WASHING

This Bible study makes a great lead-in to a service project.

For each group you'll need a clean wet towel and a clean dry towel, pens and paper, and Bibles. You'll also need one large piece of newsprint.

Have kids form groups of four; then ask each group to choose a leader. Have kids remove their shoes and give them to their group's leader. It is then each leader's responsibility to clean the shoes with the towels you provided.

While the leaders are cleaning the shoes, have groups read aloud John 13:1-17, being careful to note why Jesus washed the disciples' feet.

Bring everyone together and ask the leaders who washed the shoes:

- What were you thinking while you washed the dirty shoes?
- How did your serving compare or not compare with how Jesus served his disciples?

Ask the groups:

- How big of a deal was it that Jesus, God in human flesh, washed the feet of his disciples?
- What does Jesus' example say to us about how we should serve others?
- Have you ever served someone "lower" in position or status?
- What sometimes prevents us from doing this?
- What was Jesus showing his disciples by washing their feet?

Ask kids how they might "wash others' feet" and thereby show them love. List kids' ideas on the newsprint. Close by challenging kids to look for opportunities to love others through serving.

James Nugent
Greenwood, South Carolina

23. BIBLE NATURE SCAVENGER HUNT

This is a fun, quick, active Bible study.

Give each person or group a Bible, a list of the verses below, and a resealable bag for holding "found" items. Ask the person or group to read each Bible verse and find something in nature that represents that verse. The suggested items below are for leaders; let young people be creative in their interpretation.

- Psalm 18:2 (rock)
- Psalm 51:7 (water, soap)
- Psalm 96:12 (tree branch, bark)
- Psalm 135:6 (dirt/earth)
- Song of Solomon 2:12 (flower)
- Isaiah 4:2 (branch or fruit)
- Matthew 10:31 (feather)
- John 7:38 (water)

After everyone has gathered items, have kids explain the collections and their relation to the Scriptures. Ask:

- How is God's creation related to Scripture?
- How can these objects/items from nature help you understand Scripture?
- How do these items strengthen your connection with God?

Close by reminding kids that God's glory can be seen all around them.

Denise Prange
High Ridge, Missouri

24. THE "I" GAME

As an introduction to a Bible study about selfishness, challenge teenagers to talk without using the word *I*.

Cut index cards in half, and write the letter *I* on each one. Give each teenager three "I" cards. Tell your group that if they say "I," they must give a card to the first person who touches them. Then ask:

- Who's the most famous person you've ever met? Explain how you met him or her.
- What's the most annoying mannerism you've observed or experienced? (Don't mention any names.)
- Describe your best friend and tell one story that's a good example of how strong your friendship is.

After everyone has had a chance to talk (as well as steal cards), have students count their cards, and declare an "I" Game winner. Read aloud 1 Corinthians 10:24, and ask:

- Were you surprised by how hard it was to talk without saying "I"?
- Do you think this indicates the extent of our self-centeredness? Why or why not?
- Do you generally consider yourself to be selfish or unselfish?
- What unselfish thing can you think of that someone's done for you?
- In what way is it easiest for you to be unselfish?
- In what aspect of your life do you find it most difficult to be unselfish?

Mike Skillman
Head Waters, Virginia

25. A UNITY PROJECT

Your kids will discuss unity and work together to express the unity they hope to have with others.

Before your meeting, read Numbers 32 and Joshua 22. After kids arrive, have them read and discuss Joshua 22. Provide some background on the situation of Israel, Reuben, Gad, and Manasseh. Ask:

- What do we learn about God from this Scripture passage? about people?
- What separates believers from one another?
- What do we all have in common?

Next, discuss Christ's desire for us to have unity with other believers. Have a volunteer read John 17:20-26 and point out that Jesus prayed for this unity. Have another volunteer read Ephesians 4:1-6 and discuss what we have in common in Christ. Say: We are all very different, but we can be one. Can you picture what this would look like?

Remind your group that Reuben, Gad, and Manasseh built something to stand as a witness that the Lord was God of all of Israel even though the Jordan River separated them from the rest of the nation. Ask:

- What can we create to express to everyone (insiders and outsiders) that everyone is welcome here because of God's love?
- What kind of design would communicate that we worship and live by the instructions of a God who can make us all one even though we are very different from each other?

Allow time for kids to plan their creation. Tell kids that the plan should allow everyone to participate. Encourage kids to follow God's leading and direction, and avoid anything lame or cliché. Don't rush—this project could easily take four to six weeks.

Chip Reeves
Atlanta, Georgia

TRY THIS ONE

CROWDBREAKERS

1. BUBBLE WRAPPER

A bubble-wrapped floor will start off your meeting or event with a bang!

Collect remnants of bubble wrap over a period of time. Look for the type with large bubbles that's used to wrap furniture or computers. Before kids arrive, cover your entire meeting-room floor with the bubble wrap. When kids come in, let them run, jump, and sit on the wrap to pop all the bubbles. Continue until all the bubbles are popped. Then say, **That was noisy!** Ask:

- What are some examples of good noise and bad noise in your life?

For added fun, ask your pastor to join in on the bubble stomping!

Christine Tutak
North Hollywood, California

2. SHOW 'N' TELL GRAB BAG

Teenagers get to know each other through personal stories inspired by everyday objects.

Fill a bag with miscellaneous ordinary items, such as a comb, a match, a leaf, a toothbrush, a fork, and so on. Have your group sit in a circle, and have one student reach into the bag and take the first thing he or she touches. Give that student two minutes to tell a personal story that's related to that item. Then go around the circle until everyone has selected an item and told a story that the item brought to mind. If students have a hard time thinking of a story, suggest story themes that the items might inspire, such as a bad-hair day (comb), a campfire mishap or burning a meal (match), a nature experience (leaf), a personal hygiene faux pas (toothbrush or deodorant), or a restaurant encounter (fork). Encourage your group by going first!

Tim Hobson
Montrose, Michigan

3. HULA HEADS

This game requires little prep and will build unity among group members who don't know each other well.

You'll need at least two Hula-Hoop plastic hoops. Have kids form small groups of five to 10 people. Have groups stand in a circle, holding hands. Place a hoop around one person's neck. The object of the game is to have each team send the hoop around the circle, passing it from head to head, without kids touching it with their hands. After a few practice rounds, have teams race against each other to see who can get the hoop around the circle the quickest.

Dan and Megan Anthony
Martin, Michigan

4. PVC ROLL-OFF

Use this wild and hilarious competition to break down barriers and encourage kids to support each other—literally.

For this activity, you'll need long pieces of 3-inch PVC pipe, one pipe for every six to eight students. Make sure the pipes are long enough that there's 18 inches of pipe for each person.

Have your group form teams of six to eight, and have each team stand next to its pipe. Tell students that the team that can stand on its pipe and stay balanced for a full 30 seconds wins.

The team that will succeed is the one whose members help each other the most.

Chad Kimberly
Janesville, Wisconsin

5. NOT QUITE MUSICAL CHAIRS

This getting-to-know-you game lets teenagers share information about themselves in a fun way.

Set up chairs for the players in an inward-facing circle, but make sure there's one less chair than needed for everyone to have a seat. The person without a chair begins by standing in the middle and telling something about herself that she thinks she might have in common with others, such as "I'm an only child" or "I can play the piano." All those in the circle who share that particular characteristic must jump up and scramble to find different seats—at least two seats away from where they were sitting. The speaker rushes to grab a seat too. A new person will be without a seat, and he or she becomes the new speaker. This activity works best with a group of at least 15 or so to add a touch of chaos to the scramble in the center.

6. FAST-FOOD SAFARI

Turn an ordinary progressive dinner into getting-to-know-you fun!

Head out with your teenagers to their favorite fast-food restaurants for a memorable progressive dinner. Start with appetizers at one restaurant, move to another restaurant for drinks, still another for the main entrees, and finally a fourth restaurant for desserts. Each time you go to a restaurant, have teenagers find a different partner. When they order, have partners guess what kind of food or drink the other person will order and why they think so. For example, one partner might say, "I think you'll order water to drink because you seem to be health conscious." Be sure everyone gets a new partner at each stop.

Trisha Wilhite
Ormond Beach, Florida

7. GET-TO-KNOW-YOU TOSS

Colored balls and crowdbreaker questions are a great combination to break the ice at your next meeting.

You'll need three different colored balls for this activity. Have your group gather together in a circle, and give three people each a ball. Ask them to throw the balls to others in the circle. The participants who catch the balls must answer a question according to the color of ball they've caught. So if you have a yellow, a green, and a red ball, the person who catches the yellow ball might have to answer the questions, **"How many people are in your family, and what are their names?"** The person who catches the green ball might have to answer, **"Where do you go to school, and what subject do you like?"** The person who catches the red ball might have to answer, **"What's a fun memory or most embarrassing moment you've had?"**

Here are some other suggestions for questions:

- What's an unusual talent you have?
- What's something you're looking forward to?
- What's the craziest thing your family's ever done?

After the first three people have answered the questions, they throw the balls to three other people, who'll answer the questions according to the balls they catch. You can continue until everyone has answered at least one question.

Judy Hipes
Afton, New York

8. I NEVER...

Use a chair-swapping game to break open discussion on first impressions.

Make sure there is one chair for each teenager and that there's plenty of room for moving around. Every person takes a chair, and one person begins in the center chair, the "mush pot." That person begins by completing the sentence, "I have never..." with something he or she has never done but someone else in the circle might have done. So for example, the person in the mush pot might say, "I have never been sky diving," or "I have never been to Greenland." Instruct teenagers to keep their statements clean and to avoid embarrassing or immoral situations.

As soon as the first person makes his or her statement, anyone in the circle who has had that experience must get up and find a new chair. The last person standing has to take the chair in the mush pot. It's possible that no one will get up; in which case, the person in the middle takes another turn. Try to continue until everyone has had a chance to be in the mush pot.

The object of the game is to get to know interesting things about each other that students don't normally share. After the game, open a discussion on first impressions based on 1 Samuel 16:7.

Jennifer Tolbert
Merced, California

9. NICE TO MEET YOU

Use this simple idea to help your students make new friends quickly at a retreat or gathering.

Next time your group goes to a retreat, concert, or gathering, have T-shirts printed that read, "Nice to Meet You." Give each student a shirt to wear and some permanent markers. Encourage students to fill their shirts with signatures of the people they meet at the gathering. On the trip home, have students share stories about those they met.

Denise Prange
High Ridge, Missouri

10. PULL, POP, AND SURPRISE!

Add a bang to your New Year's activities!

You'll need to purchase party-favor crackers from a party supply store. Inside each "popper," insert a clever question, a funny quote, a Charades idea, or a Bible study question. Give one party cracker to each group member, or if you're planning a New Year's Eve dinner, place one cracker at each place setting.

Have group members take turns pulling open their party crackers. Proceed with any instruction or discussion that the cracker inserts suggest. For example, if someone pops open a Charades suggestion, be sure that person acts out that Charade. If someone receives a Bible study question or quote, allow time for discussion.

As an option, you can put additional party favors in the crackers that might relate to your current Bible study or unify your group. You might include small hearts to represent your group's love for Jesus or toy frogs to symbolize that your group is "**F**ully **R**elying **o**n **G**od."

Add this activity to a New Year's Eve party, a small-group session, or simply close your regular meeting with this fun surprise.

Michele Howe
LaSalle, Michigan

11. RUBBER-BAND FACE

Don't be afraid to try this fun crowdbreaker with your adult team!

Hand each person a large rubber band. Then instruct everyone to put the rubber band around his or her head—between the nose and upper lip, over the ears, and around the head. Got it?

Then when you say "go" have people try to get their rubber bands from where they are to below their chins without using their hands or any other object. Using tongues and teeth is allowed. The first person to get his or her rubber band below chin level wins. This creates a lot of funny faces and laughter!

Myra De Haan
Pella, Iowa

12. IS THAT YOUR NOSE?

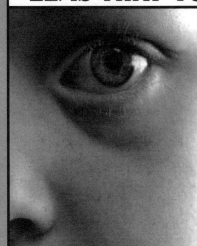

Use a digital camera to get your kids to meet each other "face to face."

Before your meeting, take several close-up pictures of your students' eyes, noses, ears, chins, and lips.

Start your meeting by projecting your pictures onto a large screen. Have students mingle to try to determine whose facial feature is on display. Have students write their guess for each image. Offer a gag prize—such as nose glasses or wax lips—to the person who has the most correct answers.

This mixer really helps a new group of students feel comfortable before the lesson begins.

Nate Stratman
Wilmington, North Carolina

13. MUSICAL CHAIRS DRESS UP

(Especially good for junior highers)

Keep group members "in fashion" in this hilarious variation of a classic crowdbreaker.

For this activity, you'll need old clothes, a CD player or radio, and chairs. Set up chairs in a large circle, facing the center. Be sure there is one fewer chair than there are participants. In the center of the circle, place a large pile of old clothes (for example, boots, hats, helmets, suits, sports equipment, dresses, shirts, shorts). You might check with a local thrift store to see if you can borrow some of the more unusual items, then return them to the store after the activity.

Begin the activity just as you would Musical Chairs, with participants walking around the circle until the music stops and then all racing to take a chair. Whoever doesn't get a chair must put on a piece of clothing from the pile in the center. Everyone gets to stay in the game! When all the clothes in the center are gone, have a fashion show!

David and Deb Wood
Hastings, Michigan

14. MONOPOLY PURSUIT

Kids will use every room in your church building for this large-group trivia game.

You'll need to make a game board similar to a Monopoly game board and designate each room or area in your church as a "property." Color-code rooms into groups of three, similar to Monopoly properties. You'll also need to create a list of trivia questions and place a volunteer in each room with one of the questions.

Have players form teams of five to seven people, and give each team a playing piece, a score card, and a map of the game board. Teams will roll dice, advance their playing pieces on the game board, and then proceed to the corresponding "property." Tell the players that the object is to make it to every room and answer all the trivia questions correctly.

Teams score 10 points for a correct answer on the first try, five points for the second try, and one point for the third try. After each correct answer, teams will return to the game board to advance to another property. If a team answers all three color-grouped properties correctly on the first try, the team scores 50 points.

Play for a set time and declare the highest-scoring team the winner, or play until a team answers all the questions.

Bryan Johnston
North Bend, Oregon

15. THE PENNY NAME GAME

This quick and easy game helps kids break down the first relationship barrier—learning other people's names.

The game starts as soon as teenagers enter the room. Have greeters welcome people and hand each person three pennies. Tell teenagers to hang onto their pennies and wait for further instructions.

Then begin your event by giving kids five minutes to introduce themselves to others and learn as many names as possible. Tell them it will be "financially beneficial" for them to play this game well.

Halfway through the evening, invite kids to continue the game by mingling again. This time through, if they remember a person's name when they greet him or her, they receive a penny from that person. (If a teenager runs out of pennies, he or she can keep on playing.) After five minutes, tally the pennies to see who remembered the most names.

If everyone in the group knows everyone else, have kids remember first and middle names or even favorite bands or TV shows. You can creatively fit this game into any meeting!

Steven Julian
Duluth, Georgia

16. T-SHIRT AFFIRMATIONS

Use T-shirt drawings as getting-to-know-you affirmations.

Hand students each a paper and pencil, and ask them to write their name at the top and draw the outline of a T-shirt. Then have students form pairs and exchange their T-shirt papers. Ask partners to interview each other about their favorite things, such as bands, TV shows, Scripture verses, food, and so on.

After five minutes, have partners design T-shirt logos for each other based on what they've discovered plus one thing they like about their partners. Once all the students have designed their T-shirt logos, have them present and explain them to the rest of the group.

Go the extra mile by having kids use markers to redraw their logos on white T-shirts.

Jenny Schneckloth
Grand Island, Nebraska

17. GIFT GIVERS

Use this idea as a way to spark friendships and inspire getting-to-know-you conversations.

Take your group to a mall, and begin a discussion about gifts and their significance. Then give each teenager the name of someone else in the group—preferably someone he or she doesn't know well. Send kids out into the mall in pairs to find gifts for their assigned people, using the following rules:

- You can't spend more than five dollars for a gift.
- You can tell only your partner who you're shopping for.
- You have to return with your gift in 30 minutes.

When teenagers have returned, have them take turns presenting their gifts to the recipients, explaining why they purchased the gifts. Ask kids to each say the following as they give their gifts: "[Name of recipient], this gift is to remind you of how valuable you are to God and to this group."

This activity works well to get kids out of their traditional meeting environment, to encourage new friendships, and to provide tokens of remembrance.

Danette Matty
Grand Island, Nebraska

18. AMIGO NIGHT

Kick off the beginning of the school year with fellowship fun!

Ask your youth group to invite all their friends to Amigo Night at your church. Tell your kids to wear old clothes to the event, but don't tell them why (they'll love the mystery). Tell them also to bring one of the ingredients needed to make taco dinners.

You might want to begin the event with a devotion about teamwork. Then talk about your youth group's upcoming activities for the next year, and pass around sign-up sheets to those interested in participating in these events. Then have kids set up a taco assembly line and make enough tacos for everyone.

After your taco dinner, have everyone go outside for a fun and messy game, such as shaving-cream volleyball (cover the volleyball with shaving cream before each serve) or Slip 'N' Slide (cover the slide with a slime product such as Yuck). Be sure to take pictures for the church newsletter!

This event is always a great way to welcome new friends and encourage fellowship.

Amy McGriff
New Sharon, Iowa

19. BIBLE TAGS

(Especially effective with junior highers)

Get kids acquainted with each other and thinking about the Bible at the same time.

Create name tags with stickers or words on them that each illustrate one of several different Bible stories. As teenagers arrive, give them name tags and explain that they're to find the others who have stickers that relate to their Bible story. (If you have extra kids, ask them to walk among the groups with a Bible and help groups learn their Bible stories if they don't know them.) After each group is complete, have one person read the Bible story while the other group members act it out.

You might use these ideas for stories and related key words or stickers:

David: slingshot, stone, giant, harp

Christmas: manger, star, angels, shepherds, wise men

Adam and Eve: apple, snake, tree, fig leaf, garden

Easter: 30 pieces of silver, soldiers, cross, tomb

Noah: ark, elephants, monkeys, worms, rainbow

Exodus: burning bush, Ten Commandments, locusts, Pharaoh

Joseph: colorful coat, pit, camels, sacks of grain

Jericho: Joshua, trumpets, walls, ram's horn

Isaac: Abraham, ram, altar, knife, thicket

Jesus feeds the 5,000: disciples; loaves of bread; fish baskets; 5,000 people

Marilyn Anderson
Bedford, Indiana

20. SPIRIT BALLOONS

Use this simple balloon activity to help kids tell each other about the Holy Spirit's action in their lives.

Give each teenager a balloon and a black marker. Have kids blow up their balloons and hold them closed at the necks without tying them. Ask teenagers to write on the balloon one place they go on a regular basis, such as school, home, library, mall, ball field, and so on.

Have the group release the balloons all at once, asking everyone to keep an eye on his or her balloon as it flies through the room. Then have everyone retrieve his or her balloon and stand wherever it landed. Ask teenagers to form groups of four or five with people who are standing closest to them.

Read aloud John 3:8. Then have kids share a short story about how they think the Holy Spirit might be active in their life. The story should relate to the location written on that person's balloon. Encourage everyone to focus on a time his or her path seemed a little crooked, like the balloons' paths when they shot off into the air.

For an added project, ask kids to write their stories on index cards, attach the cards to their balloons, and then display them on a bulletin board.

Susan Sundwall
Valatie, New York

21. WACKY QUESTIONS

This crowdbreaker is a great way to open meetings, introduce new kids, and get everyone involved.

We open every youth group meeting by having kids and adult leaders stand in a circle and state their name and a response to a bizarre question. The questions may or may not relate to our meeting topic.

The possibilities for questions are endless; we haven't run out of wacky topics yet. Here's a sampling of questions we've used:

- What's your favorite product with milk in it?
- If you were a building, what would you be?
- What's your favorite underarm deodorant and which pit do you hit first?
- What's your favorite chore around the house?
- What's the grossest food you've ever eaten?

Our kids enjoy this opening so much that they now suggest questions themselves.

Gary Toyota
Cranbrook, British Columbia

22. IF YOU WERE A ROAD SIGN

Use this opener to get kids talking about the unique characteristics God created in them and about areas of their lives that need change.

Send your young people out on the streets in groups of four, armed with Polaroid or digital cameras or paper and crayons. Challenge them to answer the question, "If you were a road sign, what would you be?" Then have kids illustrate their answers with photos or drawings of the road signs that fit their answers. Kids might find these examples:

- Slippery When Wet
- Curves Ahead
- Slow Children
- Closed to Through Traffic
- School Zone
- One Way
- Under Construction
- No Parking Any Time
- Fines Doubled for Speeding
- Do Not Pass
- Yield to Oncoming Traffic

When kids return, ask them each to explain their road sign, how it reflects who they are, and what it says about who they want to be.

Margot Hausmann
Pompton Lakes, New Jersey

23. COLD HANDS, WARM INTRODUCTIONS

In this fun activity, kids learn interesting tidbits about their partners while racing against melting ice.

Pair kids randomly with others they don't know very well. Then give each pair one piece of ice. (Make sure ice cubes are about the same size and shape.) Explain that the object of the crowdbreaker is for kids to discover as many things as possible about their partners—while melting the ice as quickly as possible. Kids must learn basic things about each other, such as name, age, school, hobbies, and talents; but they must also learn something odd, such as the color of the other person's toothbrush. If there's time, each person should find out one little-known or interesting fact about his or her partner.

Tell kids creative ice-melting techniques will be rewarded. They might rub hands, place it in their mouths, under their arms—wherever there's warmth. Have pairs signal you as soon as they ice cube is melted, and keep a list of finishers in order. When everyone is finished, have kids introduce their buddies to the large group, sharing what they discovered.

Give awards to the pair who melt their ice cube first, the person who's found the most interesting fact about his or her partner, and the pair who found the most creative way to melt an ice cube.

Ashley Pirie

24. CUT FROM A DIFFERENT DOUGH

Use sugar-cookie dough to get teenagers sharing little-known facts about themselves.

Spread store-bought rolls of sugar cookie dough into 13x9-inch pans and bake according to package directions. Bring in an assortment of cookie cutters, frostings, sprinkles, and other decorative edibles for cookies. Have kids peruse the cookie cutters and select one that characterizes them in some way. Or you can adapt this idea for the holidays by having kids select a cutter that represents or depicts a favorite part of the holiday season.

Soon after you remove the pans of cookie dough from the oven, have teenagers each cut out a cookie and take a few minutes to decorate it. Then ask kids to explain why they chose the cookie cutters they did. Encourage each person to be as specific as possible. For example, a girl might select a cookie cutter shaped like a bare foot. She might decorate the nails, put a toe ring on a toe, and frost with light brown frosting. She might explain that she likes to tan on the beach in the summer, she relaxes by painting her toenails on weekends, and she works in a jewelry store.

Add a twist to this crowdbreaker by having each person pick a group member's name out of a hat. Then have each person select a cookie cutter (or bring one to the meeting) that he or she thinks describes that person. Allow time for decoration and discussion.

Michele Howe
LaSalle, Michigan

25. NAME THAT GARGLE!

How good are your group members at translating gargle-ese? Here's how to find out.

Give group members each a glass of water, then form two teams. Have teams each think of the name of a group member on the opposite team. One team at a time gargles the name the team chose while the other team tries to guess it. Award a point to the guessers if they're correct. Have both teams gargle several names.

Then have teams think of a favorite song. One team at a time gargles its song while the others try to "Name That Gargle." Award a point to the guessing team if it guesses correctly.

Kids can gargle church or Sunday school songs ("Onward Christian Soldiers" or "Give Me Oil in My Lamp"), fairy tale songs ("Whistle While You Work" from *Snow White and the Seven Dwarfs*) or popular Christian songs ("Thy Word"). If you really want to raise the laughter level, let spectators guess the wrong song titles on purpose. Gargling team members will have a hard time containing their laughter, and will lose the water in their mouths. Have towels on hand for cleanup. Award small bottles of mouthwash for the team that guesses the most songs or the team voted "best garglers."

You could practice Christmas songs and try "gargle caroling" as a spring or summer youth group event!

Rob Rorie
Covington, Louisiana

DISCUSSION STARTERS

1. FACE-UP UNO

Here's a great way to initiate a discussion about openly sharing our faith.

Have your students form groups of six to eight people. Give each group a set of Uno cards, and have them play the game—but with all the cards in their hands facing up. Be sure that everyone in each group can see other players' cards. Play until one person in each group shouts "Uno!"

Then have groups discuss these questions:

- Why is playing Uno this way more difficult?
- How is playing Uno this way similar to the way that you share your faith? How is it different?
- What's one area of your relationship with Christ that you easily show others? What's one area that's difficult to show?
- If there were one thing about your faith that you could share with a friend who doesn't know Christ, what would it be?

Chad Kimberley
Janesville, Wisconsin

2. AGE OF THE EARTH

Use this discussion to help kids understand the relationship between faith and science.

Before your meeting, read up on some of the various theological and scientific theories about the age of the earth, and talk to your senior pastor or a science-minded person from your church. Finally, gather a list of popular celebrities and their ages.

At your meeting, play a trivia game in which youth group members guess the ages of celebrities. For every year that a player goes over the correct age, he or she receives one point. For every year that a player guesses under the correct age, he or she receives a minus point. The object is to end up with a score of zero.

After the game, ask:

- What made it hard to guess people's ages? Explain.
- How old do you think the earth is?
- Is it harder to guess the earth's age than a person's age? Why or why not?
- What various beliefs do Christians hold about the age of the earth?
- Why do you think this is a controversial topic among Christians?

Share with your students the information and opinions you've gathered. Then ask:

- How are scientific beliefs and theological beliefs alike? How are they different?
- How does science challenge your faith?
- How can you strengthen your faith when you review scientific studies or opinions?

Alfred Lu
Vancouver, British Columbia

3. INVISIBLE OBJECT LESSON

Use Kool-Aid Invisible to help generate a discussion about not judging others.

Before heading out on a weekend rally, I noticed friction between group members. For this annual trip, popular kids, new kids, bored kids, and all my other kids get mixed together and often pick on each other. I wanted to do something so the conflict wouldn't hurt the trip for my students, so I mixed up a pitcher of Kool-Aid Invisible and brought it to devotions before we left. (Kool-Aid Invisible is regular Kool-Aid drink mix made without the color. After you mix it and let it sit, it's completely clear.)

When I showed the pitcher to students, I asked them what they thought it was. When the kids answered "water," I poured everyone a cup and watched as they tasted their drinks and reacted with surprise. Then I had students keep guessing what the contents were until they figured out that they were drinking Invisible Kool-Aid. Then I asked the following:

- What decisions do you make when you see someone for the first time?
- How can those decisions hurt or help others? hurt or help ourselves?
- How do first impressions lead us to miss opportunities?
- How can we share our "flavor" of life with each other?

As a group, we decided to spend the rest of the weekend paying more attention to the "flavor" of life around us.

Isaac Arten
Escanaba, Michigan

4. ANSWERING THE CALL

Use a cell phone to spark discussion about answering God's call.

You'll need to take a cell phone with you to your youth group meeting and arrange for a volunteer to call you. Be sure he or she continues to call back until you answer the phone.

As you are discussing your lesson, let the phone ring until it stops (most cell phones only ring a limited number of times). Tell everyone to ignore the ringing, saying that if the call is important, the person will call back. When the phone rings again, continue to teach. Let the phone continue to ring until someone asks you to please answer the phone. Then ask:

- Why should I answer the phone?

After kids answer, let the phone ring one more time. This time, answer the phone, hang up, and have kids discuss these questions:

- Has God ever called you to do something and you ignored him or refused to answer? Explain.
- How do we know how to answer God's call?
- What is God calling you to do with your life?
- Why is it important to be obedient to God?
- How can you be sure to answer God's call when you hear it?

Kevin Davis
Winder, Georgia

5. TEMPTATION ISLAND

Scooters and blindfolds help launch a discussion on how sin can leave us stranded on "Temptation Island."

Have your group form two teams, and give each team a scooter and a blindfold. Use chalk to set up start and finish lines about 30 feet apart. In between, use tape and hazard cones to make a winding obstacle course for each team.

Designate one navigator for each team. Everyone else on the team is a prisoner. Have the prisoners stand at the starting line, which is known as Temptation Island. Have the navigators stand with the scooters at the finish line, which represents Victory.

On "go," the navigators must ride the scooters to Temptation Island. They each blindfold one prisoner, who then has to drive the scooter back through the obstacle course to the finish line while the navigator directs him or her with verbal commands. When they reach Victory, the navigator must go back with the blindfold and pick up another prisoner. The game continues until all prisoners are guided to Victory.

After the game, ask:

- How did it feel to have your navigator help you escape Temptation Island?
- In what ways is this game like real-life temptation?
- How does relying on each other make temptation easier to see?
- What are the best ways that someone could act as a navigator for you when you're tempted to sin? Explain.

Keith Reindl
Jackson, New Jersey

6. HEART MUSIC

Music that speaks to teenagers can elicit powerful discussion and prayer.

Set aside a regular time in your meetings when you'll listen to a song together as a group. You can allow teenagers to suggest songs, or you can plan to play popular songs that deal with issues teenagers identify with. (Be sure to preview the songs before playing them for the group.) After you play the song, talk about its effectiveness and emotional appeal. Use these questions to start a discussion, but be sure to talk about the meaning of particular lyrics:

- What words in the song speak to you? Explain.
- Do you think the song had the same meaning for the writer that it has for you? Explain.
- How does this song reflect your faith?
- How does it strengthen it?
- How might this song conflict with your faith?

After discussion, have pairs write a short prayer, asking God to help them with the feelings elicited by the song or praising God for speaking to them through the lyrics. Invite pairs to offer their prayers aloud with the group. Encourage kids to use songs on their own time as a means to connect with God.

Rebecca Kerr
Athens, Georgia

7. ANIMAL CRACKERS

Use animal crackers to spark a small-group discussion about Bible study.

Ask kids to list the names of all the animals they remember being in a box or bag of animal crackers. Then give kids bags of animal crackers, and have them note which ones they got right or wrong. Then ask:

- Do you usually look at animal crackers before eating them? Explain.
- Which could you best describe—the outside of the box or the crackers inside? Explain.
- Is this anything like your familiarity with the Bible? Why or why not?
- Can you recall specific Scripture passages that offer help, encouragement, or challenge for issues you face in everyday life?
- Have you ever offered biblical help to a friend in need? If so, how? If not, why not?

Then ask your students to brainstorm about how to find time to read God's Word during their busy days.

Amy Dowdle
Greensboro, North Carolina

8. TRADING PLACES

Taking a neighborhood tour can enlighten your teenagers about what's really important in their lives.

Before your meeting, scout out the neighborhoods in your area to find the wealthiest, most extravagant neighborhood within driving distance. For your meeting, take your youth group members on a field trip to that neighborhood. Choose several houses, and talk about what makes them elaborate and what's interesting about them. (You should avoid choosing a neighborhood where any group members reside.) Then, as you leave the neighborhood, ask everyone to be silent while one volunteer slowly reads the following verses: Psalm 49:16-20; Isaiah 5:9; Matthew 6:19-24; John 14:1-4.

After the Scripture is read aloud, stop the vehicle and discuss the following questions:

- How did you feel about these elaborate homes when we first arrived in the neighborhood?
- Did you feel differently about them after we heard the Scripture? Why or why not?
- In what ways do you place too much value on worldly possessions or status?
- How do these Scriptures challenge your priorities?

Encourage teenagers to make a commitment to focus their lives less on worldly desires and more on the things that will keep them focused on God.

Mark Wuggazer
Northville, Michigan

9. WHAT GOD SEES

This discussion on physical appearance encourages teenagers to see themselves as God's unique creations.

Give each student a 2x4-inch mirror (available at a local glass store) and modeling clay of different colors, and tell kids to use the clay to make frames or borders for their mirrors. As students design their frames, ask:

- How much time do you spend in front of the mirror each day? each week? each month?
- Why do we spend so much time worrying about how we look?
- What influences us to place so much importance on outward appearance?
- What are some ways we can safeguard ourselves from these influences?

After students have finished their mirrors, give them each a transparent mailing label or sticker with "Psalm 139" written on it, and ask each person to place the label in the middle of the mirror. Have pairs read Psalm 139 together. Then ask:

- Why is it we care about what's outside when God cares more about what's inside?
- What would help you stay focused on what's in your heart rather than on your outward appearance?

Have students keep their mirrors as visual reminders that God only cares about the beauty of their hearts.

Walter Surdacki
Campbell, California

10. FLAKES AND LOOPS

Encourage teenagers to think about how God invites us to stand out from the crowd.

Pass around a bowl of corn flakes, and ask each student to select one flake. Ask:

- How is the flake you've chosen descriptive of you?

Kids might give answers such as large, wrinkly, broken, tanned, short, uneven, or healthy. Make sure they take time to observe their flakes carefully, and then have them return their flakes to the bowl. Without them noticing, add a single piece of Froot Loops cereal and mix it in. Then have each student try to find his or her flake. Ask:

- Was it easy to find your flake? Why or why not?
- If you identified your flake, how were you able to do so?
- Did you notice anything different in the bowl this time?
- Why did the Froot Loops cereal catch your eye?

Read aloud Romans 12:2. Ask:

- How does God want us to stand out from the patterns of this world?
- What identifies us as followers of Christ? Is it hard for you to "fit in" with non-Christians? Why or why not?
- Why do you think God chooses to transform us over time instead of changing us immediately?
- How does this transformation help us better understand God's will?

Chris Cowling
Wyoming, Michigan

11. PENNY-WISE

This discussion prompts teenagers to answer the question, "Where do you spend your time?"

Give each teenager eight paper cups and 168 pennies—one penny for each hour in a given week. Have them write one of the following eight categories on each of their cups: sleeping, school, studying, family, friends, television, Internet, church, or youth group. Then ask students to place pennies in each cup equal to the number of hours in a week they spend on these activities. After everyone has finished, ask:

- Are you surprised at how your pennies were allotted? Explain.
- Did anyone have pennies left over?
- What else do you spend your time on?
- Who wished they had pennies to borrow? For what activity?
- How would you like to redistribute your time?
- How do you think God would want you to spend your time?

Encourage your kids to take the pennies home and realign their pennies daily, based on the hours they spend on each activity. Tell them to ask God to help them redistribute their time according to his will.

David Stevenson
Denver, Colorado

12. HIDDEN TREASURES

Use a safe box to spark talk about the importance of sharing God's love.

Bring a fireproof safe box filled with valuable items, such as jewelry or money, to your next meeting. Also include some items that have sentimental value, such as photos or ticket stubs. Before you open it, pass it around, and have kids speculate about what might be inside. Then open the box and reveal the contents. Ask:

- Out of all these items, which do you think is the most valuable? the most interesting?
- Which item would you choose if you could pick one thing to keep?
- Is your most treasured material possession something with monetary value or sentimental value?
- If you owned something of great value, would you keep it in a safe box?
- Would you ever take it out? Why or why not?
- What are some of the treasures that God has given us?
- Does God want us to keep these treasures "safe," or does he want us to share them with others?

This conversation is a great lead-in for a Bible study on Matthew 5:14-16; Matthew 28:18-20; or 2 Corinthians 4:7.

Julie Cheshier
Katy, Texas

13. EXTREME MAKEOVER

Even guys will have fun with this hands-on discussion about image.

For this activity, you'll need makeup, hair gel, hair spray, nail polish, and clothing from a thrift store. Form two groups, and have each group choose one person to be "made over." The group's job is to transform that person with an extreme makeover. Encourage groups to have fun and not take the makeovers too seriously. Challenge guys to let the girls give them a makeover.

When the transformations are finished, have groups discuss these questions:

- What are five reasons why people want to change who they are?
- Why does our society often turn to celebrities for the standard of how we should look?

Read aloud Genesis 1:26-27, emphasizing the word image when you read it. Ask:

- What does it mean when you hear, "Image is everything"?
- What does the world say about one's image?
- When we think of the world's definition of image, we think of what we see. When you think of being created in the image of God, what do you think of?

Close with a prayer of thanksgiving that God has created us in his image.

Scott Meier
Norman, Oklahoma

14. ANTI-SUPER-BOWL PARTY

Use this idea to change the traditional Super Bowl party into rowdy fun.

You'll need: two walkie-talkies, a TV, games or activities, a score card, a prize, one volunteer to watch the Super Bowl, at least one game leader, and, of course, food!

When kids arrive, have them form teams of at least four. Set up the TV in one room and the games and activities throughout other areas. Gather everyone around the TV, and start the activities right after the national anthem. Give your game leader one walkie-talkie, and give the other one to the volunteer who's watching the TV. Have teams play their first game until the TV-watching volunteer informs them via the walkie-talkie that the first commercials are on. Whoever is ahead in the game wins a point, and the first team to make it to the TV room gets a point. The first team that guesses what product a commercial is advertising also gets a point. After the commercials, teams will go to their next game until the next set of commercials comes on. Continue the games until the Super Bowl is over.

Afterward, discuss:

- If you were going to advertise yourself to millions of people, what would you say?
- If you could advertise God, what would you say?

Tyler Dunlap
Perrysburg, Ohio

15. BROWNIE MIX LESSON

Use a variety of brownie mixes to launch a discussion on following God's plan.

For this discussion starter, you'll need the use of a kitchen, and you'll need to buy a different brand of brownie mix (and other needed ingredients) for every three to four people. If you have a large group, you can assign multiple groups to the same brand of brownie mix.

Form groups of three or four, and name each group according to its brand of brownie mix—Pillsbury, Duncan Hines, and Betty Crocker, for example. Allow each group time to make brownies.

While brownies are baking, challenge each group to brainstorm and present a quick object lesson based on its brownie mix and to back up its lesson with Scripture. They might use the "guarantee" message on their boxes to talk about God's promises, they might talk about mixing together ingredients as an analogy for church unity, or they might talk about "the right ingredients" for forgiveness.

When the brownies are finished, have the group taste-test them and vote on the best recipe. Then discuss:

- How is following a brownie recipe like following God's will?
- Is it easier to follow a brownie recipe or God? Explain.
- How can someone improve his or her baking skills?
- How can we improve our ability to follow God's calling?

Diana Hartman
Pittsburgh, Pennsylvania

16. WHICH CELEBRITY AM I?

Generate a good discussion on how to strengthen our identity in Christ.

Before your meeting, write the names of several different celebrities on separate index cards. Have kids form teams of four or five, and have each team select someone to be the "celebrity." Give each celebrity an index card with a celebrity's name on it, and tell him or her not to show it to the rest of the team. Then the team will begin asking yes or no questions to guess who its celebrity is. Instruct the celebrities to answer the first question either as themselves or as the celebrities. Then they must alternate each answer after that between what they'd say and what their celebrities would say. The other team members will have to discern which answers pertain to the teenagers and which ones pertain to the celebrities. The first team to figure out who the celebrity is wins! After the game, have the teams discuss these questions:

- How did you figure out when an answer was the celebrity's and when it was your teammate's?
- Do you think in real life people sometimes give responses that aren't really their own? Why or why not?
- How do we know what's really true in people's hearts? in our own hearts?
- Does what you say to others reflect your relationship with Christ? Explain.
- How can you remember your relationship with Christ when you respond to others?

John Wilkinson
Bethlehem, Pennsylvania

17. THE RACE IS ON

Use video games to initiate discussion about competition and spiritual growth.

Set up a video game system with a car-racing game and controls for four players. If you don't have one, you might try borrowing one from a student or a church member.

Have your group form four teams, and have each team pick a driver to go first. Allow these four players to compete in a short race.

Encourage other teammates to cheer for their drivers.

Once the race ends, have a mock interview with the winning driver, asking how he or she pulled out the big win. Allow four new drivers to play another round, and continue playing as time allows.

Then ask:

• What draws people to sports competitions?

• In what other ways do people compete against each other?

• In general, how competitive are you?

• In what area of life are you the most competitive?

Read aloud 1 Corinthians 9:24-27. Ask:

• Does it seem appropriate to express a competitive drive in our spiritual lives? Why or why not?

• Who or what are we competing against in this area?

• What type of spiritual training do you think is most effective in creating spiritual growth?

• To what extent are you competitive or aggressive about your spiritual training?

Chad Kimberley
Janesville, Wisconsin

18. ARE THE STARS OUT TONIGHT?

A stardom role-play teaches teenagers why God deserves our praise above all others.

Before your meeting, purchase magazines that have large photos of current pop culture icons. They can be movie stars, musicians, sports figures, TV stars, or even cartoon characters. Cut out the photos of the pop stars and glue each of them on cardboard. Then attach the pop stars to craft sticks to create stick puppets.

Tell your group that there are many famous people competeing for our praise and attention, and you've brought a few of them with you. Hand out the stick puppets, and ask teenagers to take turns holding up their icons and "performing" like that star might in real life. Have each person tell why his or her pop star is most special. Then take a vote—by applause—on which pop star really deserves the most praise.

After the activity, have pairs discuss these questions:

• When it comes to famous people today, whom do you admire the most? Explain.

• Why do people worship pop stars like those we discussed?

• What is worship?

• Why do we worship God?

Close by talking about why God is the one who deserves our worship above all others.

John Pape
Kettering, Ohio

19. PIZZA PRAISE

Generate good discussion with something teenagers love best—pizza!

This discussion starter works great for a pizza party or lock-in. For this event, you'll need pizza dough and tomato paste. Ask kids to bring their favorite pizza toppings.

Before you begin making pizzas, read aloud a psalm that discusses creation, such as Psalm 8, 104, or 148. Ask everyone to take a few moments of quiet time to reflect on the psalm. Then have kids form groups of four to make pizzas. Instruct students to use their toppings to express something about God's creation that came to mind during their quiet time. They might make a fish with pepperoni scales and sliced green pepper for waves, or flowers or trees made from tomato slices and strips of green pepper.

While pizzas are in the oven, begin a discussion on creation with these questions:

- Why do you think God made the world the way he did?
- What's your favorite thing that God made? Explain.
- How do you fit in as a part of God's creation?
- How does God reveal himself to you through his creation?

Petrea Facey
Kingston, Jamaica

20. THE IMPORTANCE OF BEING PURE

Recruit courageous and faith-strong guys to impact a discussion on purity.

Use this idea when you have a girls-only session on purity. Before you begin your regular meeting, let girls know that a few new girls will be visiting but are running late. Recruit some brave guys to dress up as girls, burst into the meeting, and announce they're on the hunt for some cute guys. Allow them five minutes to describe what they look for in guys, what they don't look for, and how they'd go about getting their guys. If you have more time, allow girls to ask these "ladies" additional questions about their dating habits.

After five minutes allow the "girls" to leave, return to their original clothes, and then rejoin the meeting. Ask the guys to share with the girls why purity is important to them and why a girl who's strong in her faith is important to them. Then have the group discuss the following questions:

- What's the most important quality you look for in a guy or girl? the least important quality?
- How important is appearance to you?
- How important is purity to you?
- Would you compromise your beliefs or standards for someone you might date? Explain.

Be sure that the guys participate in the discussion along with the girls. Hearing opinions on purity from female role models is effective, but hearing those opinions from cute guys will have maximum impact and create a great dialogue.

Danette Matty
Grand Island, Nebraska

21. NUTS AND BOLTS

Here's a fun way to divide large groups into smaller discussion groups.

Collect enough nuts and bolts so that you have one nut and bolt for every two people. Choose several different-sized sets of nuts and bolts, and make sure you have four or five sets of each size. Mix all the nuts and bolts, and when teenagers arrive, give each person either a nut or a bolt.

Have young people introduce themselves to each other as they try to find the match to their nuts or bolts. When they find a match, they'll continue to look for others who have the same size nuts or bolts as they do. Everyone continues to mingle until all the small groups have found all their members.

Then ask the groups to discuss the following:

- How does finding similarities with each other make our group stronger?
- What are the nuts and bolts of our youth ministry?

After a few minutes of discussion, ask:

- What are the nuts and bolts of your faith?
- How are the essentials that make up our youth ministry related to the essentials that make up our faith?
- What can we do together to strengthen our faith that we can't do alone?

Let teenagers keep their nuts and bolts as reminders of the importance of our connection to each other.

Paul Farrell
Hartland, Wisconsin

22. LETTING GO OF THE WEIGHTS

This "heavy" activity will help teenagers think about how to survive hardships.

You'll need Bibles, tape, two pouches that strap around the waist, sand or rocks, paper strips, and pens.

Fill the pouches with sand or rocks, and have a volunteer read aloud Hebrews 12:1. Ask:

- What's the difference between weights and sins?
- What are some things that might be "weights" in your life?

Pass out two paper strips and a pen to each group member, and have them each write an example of sin on one strip and an example of a weight on the other. Tape the paper strips to the pouches. Ask another volunteer to strap the pouches around his or her waist and run two laps around the room. Ask:

- How does it feel to run with all that extra weight?

Then have the volunteer remove the pouches and run laps around the room again. Ask:

- How does it feel to run now?

Have the group separate into trios and read 2 Timothy 2:3-4. Have trios discuss these questions:

- What hardships do you face by being a Christian?
- How important is it to free yourselves from other weights?
- How can you keep worldly struggles from interfering with your spiritual life?

Roger Prewitt
Monroe, Michigan

23. SCAVENGERS WITH A MISSION

This scavenger hunt will help your kids have fun, serve the community, and reflect on some important issues concerning poverty.

Before your meeting, recruit several adult drivers and make a list of items to be retrieved by each team. Each item on the list needs to be some sort of basic food or toiletry item, such as bread, rice, canned goods, toothpaste, diapers, and so on. Assign a separate point value to each item. Photocopy lists for each team and obtain several fast-food gift certificates to give away as prizes.

Once your group is assembled, have kids form teams and assign each team to a driver. Explain that their goal is to collect the most points and return to the meeting place within a given time frame.

Give each team a small amount of money—$10 to $15—less than they'd need to purchase every item on the list. Also explain the following rules:

(1) The team can't spend more money (including tax) than what you give them; They must bring back the receipt as proof;

(2) No team can visit the home of any church or youth group member;

(3) After their money runs out, each group will have to be creative in obtaining the remaining items; and

(4) Obtaining any item by any illegal or unethical means is, of course, prohibited.

After tallying the final scores, announce the winner and reward the members of the team with the fast-food certificates. Ask:

• What was it like to go into a store knowing that you had more items on the list than you could afford?

• If you were a low-income single parent who couldn't afford everything on the list, how would you prioritize?

• Where would someone go in real life if he or she couldn't afford necessities?

Read aloud Matthew 25:31-46. Ask:

• Who are the "least of these"?

• Why does Jesus pay special attention to the "least of these" in these verses?

• What should our motivation be for helping the "least of these"?

• How does helping others change us?

Wrap up by announcing that all of the items collected in the hunt will either be donated to a local shelter or given to needy families in your church. Determine a day when kids can drop the items off.

Also challenge the winning team members to carry their certificates with them and to give them away the next time someone solicits them for money or food.

Scott Bomar
Los Angeles, California

24. FLICKS AND FOOD

Turn a progressive dinner into a progressive discussion starter on faith, hope, and love.

At church and at two homes, you'll watch movie clips and have discussions while you eat. Start the progressive dinner at church and watch the segment from *Toy Story* in which Buzz "proves" he can fly. Talk about faith and how important it is to accomplishing goals. (Scripture link: Matthew 17:20; clip location: 29:45 through 31:00.)

At the first house, watch the segment from *Castaway* in which Chuck talks about clinging to hope when things seem hopeless. Talk about the way hope works together with and strengthens faith. (Scripture link: 2 Thessalonians 2:16-17; clip location: 2:09:00 through 2:12:15.)

At the last house, watch the segment from *Austin Powers: The Spy Who Shagged Me* in which Dr. Evil bounces a rubber globe off Number Two's face. Compare the way people treat each other with the way God loves each of us. Talk about how love works together with faith and hope. (Scripture link: Luke 6:27-36; clip location: 50:45 through 51:30.)

Use Scripture to reassure teenagers that God loves them, that your group loves them, and that you will be there for them during tough times to show them faith, hope, and love.

Candace Ingle
North Wilkesboro, North Carolina

25. SEEK AND PRAY

In this activity, kids discern the value and purpose behind familiar organizations and places in their community. But first they have to find them.

Before your group meeting, use a digital camera to take pictures of familiar objects and places in your community. However, take pictures of only a portion of each, such as the chain of a park swing, the door of a school, or half of a sign. At your meeting, form groups of three or more, and give each group the same five to 10 photos. Mix up the order of the photos for each group, and tell groups they must find the objects in the order given. This will ensure that groups get to each venue at different times.

Then have groups go out into your community to find the objects in the pictures. Once each object is found, have groups answer these questions:

- What purpose does this place or organization serve in our community?
- How is our community benefited by this place or organization?
- How would our community be different without it?

After answering the questions, have group members pray for the organization or place. For example, if kids end up at a school, they could pray for teachers, students, and outreach possibilities there.

After a set amount of time, return to the church and have groups share their experiences.

Randy McKain and Jeff Anderson
Bemidji, Minnesota

TRY THIS ONE

FUND-RAISERS

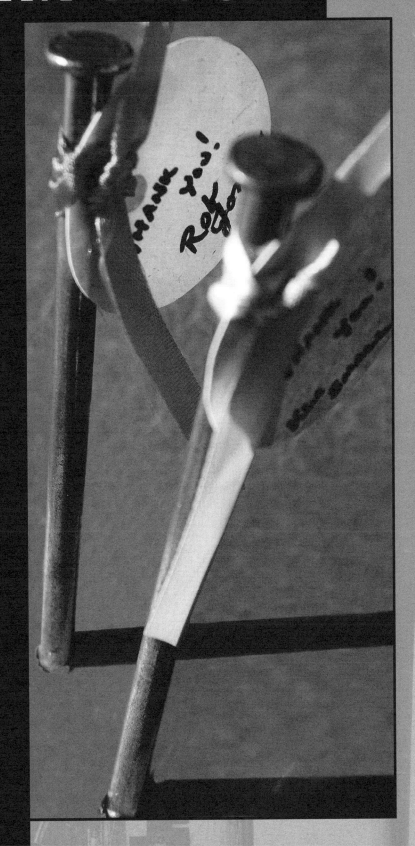

TRY THIS ONE

1. NO-FUSS FUND-RAISERS

With these great fund-raising ideas, no one has to ask a single congregation member to buy anything!

We're currently in a building program, which means that extra youth funds don't exist, and we're not supposed to solicit money from the congregation. So we've started to raise money through recycling. Kids collect old soda cans for about 50 cents a pound and empty computer printer ink-jet cartridges, which can be sold for about $2 each. (Try using a printer cartridge recycling Web site such as www. empties4cash.com.)

Best of all, we've been collecting old cell phones and getting about $3 each. (Try Web sites such as www.ecophones.com or www. wirelessredemption.com.) We've called every cell phone store in our area and regularly receive 100 or more a month. Here's the cool part—we sell the working cell phones on Ebay, getting as little as $3.50 to as much as $120 for each phone. It requires very little effort and students are doing most of the work. We've made more than $4,000 in the past one and a half years!

Mark Wilhoite
Fort Worth, Texas

2. YOUR CHURCH'S FUNNIEST HOME VIDEO

Involve your church families in this wild media event.

You'll need a video camera and permission from its owner to allow kids to operate it. Train two or three kids to be the official camera operators.

Choose 12 families in your church to participate in making a "movie." Schedule appointments with families in their homes. Use a 90-minute videotape to consecutively tape the five-minute segments. When your film crew arrives at each family's house, have the crew choose one of the scenarios listed below for the family to act out in no more than five minutes. (Don't tell the family ahead of time what they'll be doing.) .

The scenarios:
- getting arrested for laughing too loud
- holding a funeral for an inanimate object
- getting married in a bathroom
- robbing a piggy bank
- building a "Dagwood" sandwich with unusual items
- everyone preparing for bed and sleeping in a twin bed
- making a commercial to sell the oddest object in the house
- a guided tour of the refrigerator
- a "pool" party in the bathtub
- singing a song—backward
- catching a dirty-laundry thief
- a fashion show with each family member wearing other family members' clothes

Schedule a premiere showing of the completed video. Charge a small fee, and sell refreshments.

Michael Capps
East Flat Rock, North Carolina

3. HELPING HANDS

Instead of a traditional bake sale, make creative hand cookies to earn money for your next service project.

Plan to have a baking party with your group the night before your next bake sale. A few weeks before your bake sale, publicize your fund-raiser by selling paper hand cutouts called "Helping Hands." Let people know they can lend a helping hand to your group's next service project without lifting a single hammer or breaking a sweat. The paper hands act as coupons to be redeemed for artistically decorated cookies specially designed by youth group members.

At your baking party, have your youth group bake and decorate hand-shaped cookies. You can find hand-shaped cookie cutters in a gourmet kitchen store or from Web sites such as www.wilton.com or www.kitchenkrafts.com. Have teenagers use their creativity to uniquely frost and decorate their cookies. Encourage them to add Christian symbols such as rainbows, crosses, doves, peace symbols, and hearts. Place each cookie on a small paper plate and cover it with plastic wrap to hand out at the bake sale the next day.

Be sure to make a few extra cookies in case of "finger" breakage, and enjoy broken fingers with milk as you clean up the kitchen!

Rachel Gilmore
Frankfort, Illinois

4. CARHOP CONCESSIONS

Take your community back to the '50s for food, music, and fun!

Schedule a time that the youth ministry can use the church's parking lot for this fund-raiser. Recruit adult volunteers to prepare the food and drinks. Plan to serve hamburgers, hot dogs, chicken-breast sandwiches, french fries, nachos, soft drinks, root beer floats, and hot fudge sundaes. Come up with creative '50s-style names for your menu, such as Big Bopper Burgers and Hot Diggety Dogs.

Set up a CD player and play '50s rock 'n' roll. Have the young people work as carhops, dressed in poodle skirts and sweaters, cuffed jeans and T-shirts, or leather jackets, and have as many kids as possible wear skates while they take orders and serve people. You can set up tables and chairs for those who don't want to eat in their cars.

We hold this fund-raiser every September, and many of our "customers" even bring out their old Mustangs, Thunderbirds, or other old cars!

Terri Brown
Alva, Oklahoma

5. DONATION LETTER

Let's face it. Most people who support youth group fund-raisers don't need more candy, wrapping paper, or carwashes. They just want to help your young people. So the next time you need to raise money for a trip, why not simply send letters to ask for donations?

Use your church letterhead for a letter explaining the purpose of your trip, how much each individual must raise, what your plans for the trip are, and how it will benefit the group members and their faith lives. Include information about where to send a check and how it should be made out. Give youth group members about 20 to 25 letters each, and have them add personal notes at the bottom. Don't mention any specific amount, but you can expect about $20 from each person who receives a letter—and the amount is often much greater.

Be sure to keep track of all those who donate, and have the teenagers send thank-you notes and photos from the trip afterward.

Chris Coletti
Vista, California

6. LOVE BUG

Send out your "cupids" on Valentine's Day to deliver special gifts as a seasonal fund-raiser.

Six weeks prior to Valentine's Day, start advertising that the Love Bug is coming! Then three to four weeks before Valentine's Day, start taking orders for delivery of $10 or $15 gifts. These might be glass candy dishes or large sundae glasses filled with candy. We've also used nice frames and included photos of a loved one. For kids at school, deliver small bags of goodies and charge only $5. Have senders add Valentine messages to be delivered with the gifts. Helium balloons can also be added. As an option, provide a singing message or poem for an additional charge.

Your Love Bug delivery program will grow each year as the word gets around in your community and people discover this less-expensive alternative to sending flowers.

Gary Townsend
Dublin, Georgia

7. APRIL SHOWERS AND MAY FLOWERS

Combine two fund-raisers into a missions project that plants hope for local orphans or homeless kids.

Encourage your youth group members to collect pledges from family, friends, and congregation members. Ask those who pledge to give a certain dollar amount each time it rains or snows in April. At the end of April, collect those donations. Then in May, work with a local florist who can give your youth group a discount on flower orders for Mother's Day. Make arrangements to have your youth group members deliver the flower orders on Mother's Day.

With the money that's raised, contribute to a local orphanage or shelter for homeless kids. Throw those kids a "shower" in which you bring sweet treats, play games, and sing songs. At the end of your shower, present the funds you raised to the director of the organization.

Karla Kaphaem
Neenah, Wisconsin

8. YOUTH MISSION-A-THON

This pledge-based event builds teamwork and enthusiasm for your group's missions trip.

For your next missions trip fund-raiser, plan a "youth mission-a-thon" in which your students run or walk the marathon distance of 26.2 miles—as a group. Before the event, have teenagers collect "per mile" pledges from sponsors. For example, friends and family might pledge $1 per mile for a total of $26 or 50 cents per mile for a total of $13. Encourage each teenager to seek at least four sponsors.

Reserve a park or track beforehand, and ask volunteers to hand out water and snacks. Have all the teenagers set out on the course together to cover their designated share of the 26.2 miles. (For example, if you have 26 students, they'd each have to cover one mile.) Encourage family and friends to gather along the route to cheer on the runners/walkers.

Kids have a great time with this team effort, and your group can generate a large sum of money in a short period of time with little preparation.

Tony Akers
Huntsville, Alabama

9. BALLOON-A-GRAMS

Raise money and help your church spread encouragement!

You can make this Valentine Balloon-A-Gram sale an annual fund-raiser. You'll need about two tanks of helium, card stock for 3x5-inch cards, curling ribbon, heart candy, mesh fabric, and plenty of balloons. Have your group design cards with hearts or Valentine's Day art in the right corner and then add the labels "To:" and "From:" for the Balloon-A-Gram senders to fill out. Also leave as much space as possible on the cards for the senders to write messages.

You can sell Balloon-A-Grams for about $1 per balloon. Tie a mesh bag filled with candy hearts, along with the card, to the bottom of the balloons for weight. Be sure to offer customers more than one balloon for each card, if they like.

On the Saturday before delivery, have your group make the candy mesh sacks, adding strings for the number of balloons to be attached. On the morning of delivery, gather your group at 7 to inflate balloons and attach them to the cards. A good time to plan your delivery is at the beginning of Sunday school before Valentine's Day.

Our group spends about $250 for this fund-raiser, but we raise more than $1,200 each year.

Jeff Cops
Murfreesboro, Tennessee

10. OUR FAVORITE RESTAURANT

Raise money and build fellowship in your congregation—with little effort.

This low-energy, high-yield fund-raiser worked well with a large, popular restaurant in our community. Holding the event at a popular restaurant made sales a lot better than hosting a spaghetti dinner. We sent a letter to a local restaurant announcing our intentions for a fund-raiser and asked the restaurant for its participation. Then we followed up with a meeting. We chose a Mexican restaurant since the money was going to fund a trip to Mexico. The restaurant manager agreed to host a buffet lunch for up to 300 people.

We printed and sold tickets to both congregation members and the community for $15 each. The restaurant collected $3.50 per ticket, charged for beverages, and used the event as a tax write-off. We netted $4,000, with little preparation! The restaurant enjoyed the publicity and news coverage, and the congregation enjoyed a great lunch and interaction with the community.

Jim Miller
Honolulu, Hawaii

11. PIE AUCTION

Dig in to a tasty and lucrative fund-raising favorite!

Ask your teenagers and their parents to provide pies for sale. Publicize your auction and hold it one hour before a regularly held meeting, such as a quarterly congregational meeting, a volunteer recruiting meeting, or after a midweek worship service. Recruit a local auctioneer to emcee the pie auction. Have your youth group members serve ice cream, lemonade, and coffee to guests as they arrive.

To present the items for auction, ask a teenager or youth group sponsor to hold up a pie while other teenagers record the bids. Encourage your youth group members to pool their money and bid against the adults. When the youth group wins a pie, have everyone grab a fork and dig right in!

This is a fund-raising favorite because it takes little preparation and everyone has a great time. Our record single-pie sale was $70!

Kim Wills
Pella, Iowa

12. CHOCOLATE AT WORK

Use a new, easy, and cheap fund-raiser to support your summer missions trips.

Purchase a large quantity (a case or more) of mini M&M's candies in tubes. On a Sunday morning, hand out the tubes of M&M's to church members as they exit after a service. Tell everyone that instead of selling candy, your group is giving it away. As you hand out the candy, encourage people to take the tubes home, eat the candy, and then fill the empty tubes with quarters (a tube will hold about $14 worth of quarters). Tell church members that M&M's stands for "missions money," and ask them to pray for your missions trip every time they add quarters to the tubes. When a tube is filled, a church member can return it to your group. Your group's time and effort will be minimal with this fund-raiser; plus, you'll have church members praying for your missions trip every time they see or eat M&M's.

Michael Haley
Pueblo, Colorado

13. THE APPRENTICE

It's tough to get your teenagers to show up for an event that's billed as a fund-raiser. Instead, invite them to participate in an Apprentice game that involves real money and a fun competition.

Have your youth group form two teams, and tell teams that you're challenging them to raise money without any startup capital. Teams should each elect a project manager to oversee the task. Teams must come up with their own means by which they'll raise money, and they're challenged to beat the other team in the amount of funds they raise. Teams will need to determine whom they'll target for their projects, how they'll do them, and when they'll conduct their fund-raising events. Assign teams a final date by which their task must be accomplished. Then gather both teams together at that date to discuss the successes of their fund-raising efforts.

We gave our teams the task of putting on a yard sale. Kids came up with the location, sale items, and advertisements. One team made a special effort to collect the best quality products and then enlisted church members to bake homemade desserts. To top it off, they obtained a prime location for their sale by talking the local fairground management into waiving the $100 rental fee. The other team solicited donations for lunch supplies and sold lunches to the sale shoppers.

This fund-raiser was wildly successful for our church, raising $1,400—double what we'd expected to raise!

Mike Kirby
Powhatan, Virginia

14. BOWL AND BOWL

Bring your entire church together for fun and fellowship with this fund-raising event.

This event is simple to plan and deliver. Sell tickets to your congregation and community for an afternoon of bowling followed by a "bowl" potluck: a meal of anything served in bowls! First, plan the event by reserving several lanes at your local bowling alley. Next, have youth group members sign up to prepare any type of food that's served in a bowl, such as chili, soup, stew, or bread-bowl dips. Although adult leaders and parents can help, be sure the teenagers take main responsibility for preparing and serving dinner, as well as cleaning up.

Use the after-dinner coffee and dessert time to present wacky awards for bowling—for example, lowest score, highest score, best celebration for a strike, or most gutter balls.

Jason Grootenboer and Rick Kramer
Kingston, Ontario

15. CARWASH SPONSORS

Every youth group has held a carwash fund-raiser. But here's how you can make it really lucrative.

The next time you hold a carwash fund-raising event, take a few extra steps to increase your profit by getting other businesses involved. First create a letter on church letterhead to explain the purpose of your youth group's fund-raiser and send it to local businesses, asking them to sponsor the event with donations. Tell them that in exchange for the donations, they'll receive free advertising for their businesses during the carwash. Have youth group members collect the sponsoring companies' business cards and then create a flier that lists all the sponsors. Make sure every carwash customer receives a flier with his or her wash.

This is a great way to add more profit to your fund-raising event with little expense.

Toby Roehm
Winter Haven, Florida

16. COOKIE CHRISTMAS CARDS

"My group has done this fund-raiser twice...with great results!"

In early December, have your kids take orders from your congregation for Chocolate Chip Cookie Christmas Cards. Make order forms with spaces for the following information: buyer's name and phone number; receiver's name, address, and phone; quantity; a short greeting from the sender; and total dollars due. Explain to buyers that recipients will receive a homemade cookie and a greeting from them (the buyer) for a modest price ($2 is reasonable). Be sure to have kids explain how they'll use the funds; we used ours to buy Christmas presents for needy children in our community.

On a designated night, prepare the cookies at the church kitchen or at a group member's home. Make traditional round cookies, or bake dough in a pan and cut out shapes with Christmas cookie-cutters immediately after the dough has cooled. Have kids write the greetings from the senders on small pieces of colored paper or construction paper and attach them to the cookies. Then have kids package the cookies attractively and hand-deliver them to the receivers.

Jim Galbraith
Prince Rupert, British Columbia

17. IN THE BAG

If you need to quickly raise big bucks for a summer mission trip or other event, this is the idea for you.

The idea is simple: Have your group bag groceries for tips on Super Bowl weekend. We did this and made $1,050! Here's how to ensure success.

Talk with the manager at your local discount grocery store or Wal-Mart Supercenter. Your services are especially welcome at stores such as these because they typically don't employ full-time baggers. Your kids can simplify the cashiers' job and help lines move more quickly. And, if you go with Wal-Mart, you may get an added bonus—many stores will match raised funds up to $1,000! Talk with the store manager about this program.

Tell the manager your group would like to provide a service for them and, at the same time, raise funds for your group. Also, explain that your kids will work at all registers throughout the day, wear name badges, and collect tips only at the entrances and exits of the store.

Make name badges that include your church's name, the group member's name, the phrase "Bagging for Tips," and what your funds will be used for—for example, a Mexico trip fund-raiser. The badges can be as simple or elaborate as you want, but make them uniform. If your group has T-shirts with your group or church name on them, have kids wear these as well. Make larger versions of the name badge to outfit large coffee cans, which will act as your tip receptacles. Make sure the coffee can signs look the same as the name badges to aid recognition.

Before heading to the grocery store, go over bagging basics with your kids. Also remind them this is a service project as well as a fund-raiser, so they should come with their best attitude and, of course, smile!

Nate Ferguson
Morris, Illinois

18. PALATE-PLEASING MONEYMAKER

Make some cool summer cash with this easy idea.

Look in your local yellow pages under "ice cream" for wholesale distributors in your area. Call them and let them know you'd like to sell ice cream as a fund-raiser for your youth group. They'll likely sell you the ice cream for a very reasonable price so that you can sell it for a profit. Sell the ice cream at any special church event, such as a picnic or barbecue, or sell it in the parking lot after your Sunday service.

At a church picnic, we sold four different flavors of ice cream for $1 per cone or cup and made $99 profit in about 15 minutes! It was the easiest way to beef up the youth budget we've ever tried.

Tim Kemptner
Manteca, California

TRY THIS ONE

19. RAISE THE ROOF

This mission trip fund-raiser hits the nail on the head!

To raise funds for our Group Workcamp Foundation missions trip, in which we fix up homes for the elderly, the disabled, or fixed-income families (www.groupworkcamps.com), we had an adult leader build a small 4x5-foot "house" that looked similar to a manger. We drilled a thousand holes in the roof, and then we sold nails for $1.00 each. Our youth group tied every nail with a brightly colored ribbon and attached a small tag, thanking the sponsor.

We asked church members to buy nails, write their names on the tags, and place their nails in the roof's holes. We left the display up for four months, and the roof slowly filled with brightly colored "shingles." We had more than enough money for our missions trip!

Pam Gjersvig
Stevens Point, Wisconsin

20. LIFE CHANGERS

Pennies, nickels, dimes, and quarters add up to big bucks with this easy fund-raiser.

To raise funds for a mission trip, we set up a display titled, "Your Small Change, Changing Lives." We mounted four clear plastic tubes to the display, one for each type of coin—pennies through quarters. At 4-to-5-inch increments all the way up the tubes, we wrote the dollar amount each tube would hold at that level. We also placed sealed envelopes, each with a different fact about world hunger, at various levels. (You can customize the facts to fit your trip. Visit the "kids can make a difference" Web site at www.kidscanmakeadifference.org for hunger facts.) When the coins in a tube reached an envelope, we opened the envelope and displayed the fact for all to enjoy.

We asked church members to consider dropping their pocket change into the tubes every time they walked by the display. We kept the display up until we left for our trip four months later.

Julie Brewer
Humble, Texas

21. CHOCOHOLIC SUNDAY

This favorite fund-raiser is profitable, fun, and delicious.

Kids get together for two hours the day before the fund-raiser and make chocolate desserts, such as brownies, cookies, and cakes.

We usually schedule this event for the same Sunday evening as one of our church's quarterly business meetings. And we add to the plethora of sweet indulgences by inviting church members to bring their favorite chocolate desserts, too. The kids serve the desserts, collect donations, and wrap up post-event leftovers for our local rescue mission.

Lena Wellman
Casper, Wyoming

22. I CAN SEE CLEARLY NOW

Finding good fund-raisers where adults aren't making a contribution just to be nice can be almost impossible. After trying nearly every fund-raiser known to man, our most successful project has turned out to be—washing windows.

We started with a simple sign-up poster at church. We offered to do windows for $1 each, inside and out. Before long, word spread to the larger community, and we ended up with more requests than we could accept. We provided a real service and raised more than enough money for a 19-day mission trip to Mexico.

Additional benefits included wonderful publicity for our mission trip and valuable experience in team building. Kids shared responsibilities for cleaning, inspections, and problem-solving: "How do we get to that window?" By the time we embarked on our trip, kids had a high level of confidence in their ability to work together.

Robert Coombs
Norris, Tennessee

23. GIVING GOOD GIFTS

Want to encourage service while giving your youth budget a boost? Try one of these win-win ideas.

1. Put together a service directory that includes the names and phone numbers of everyone in your youth ministry. List people according to a service they're capable of providing, such as baby-sitting, yardwork, painting, housecleaning, and car washing. Church members can call kids for specific jobs and make donations for the tasks performed.

2. Involve your church in a silent auction that showcases people's abilities and supports the youth group. Ask the whole congregation—especially youth group members—to do some soul searching about their God-given talents or gifts that might benefit others. These can range from professional skills (tax-return assistance from a CPA) to hobbies (tennis lessons from an enthusiast) to possessions (a weekend in a vacation cabin from its owner).

Publicize the silent auction throughout the church and community after choosing an ideal date and time. Participants will enjoy the fellowship and bargain hunting. You can also add a free-will-offering spaghetti meal afterward. Our group raised more than $1,000 and incurred only $50 of expenses.

David Burger
Catlin, Illinois
Marnie Childs
Norman, Oklahoma

24. CAPPUCCINO STAND

As every youth leader knows, fund-raisers can be a real headache. But I believe we've found one that really works and generates more benefits than we bargained for.

You'll need a blender or two, an ice chest, a table, and cappuccino supplies: cappuccino powder mix, milk, ice, whipped cream, chocolate syrup, chocolate sprinkles, and cups. Your group can sell hot drinks in the winter and iced cappuccinos in the summer (directions for each are on the powdered mix container). Set up shop in your fellowship area, and then look for these great results:

- The kids in your group raise their own support and learn to be responsible.
- It's a high-profile fund-raiser. Congregation members who aren't familiar with your youth ministry will be delighted to see what "their church" is doing.
- The kids meet and build relationships with adults who could have a positive influence on them.
- It's a reason for church members to hang around and mingle more than they would otherwise, resulting in feelings of belonging.
- The investment is minimal.
- It's largely run by kids, with minimum effort required from adult leaders.

You may find some in your congregation are more willing to sponsor kids for camps and events after they see your kids' willingness to "earn their own keep."

What starts out as a fund-raiser may grow into a ministry.

Brad Miller
San Bernardino, California

25. FAST FUNDS

This simple fund-raiser has several benefits: no overhead cost, very little administrative work, easy publicity, whole-church involvement, and spiritual growth and uplift.

List all the meals that will happen while your youth group is on an upcoming mission trip. On a Sunday about a month beforehand, give a brief presentation to the entire congregation about the trip, explaining its purpose. Then ask everyone to support you by praying and fasting for the trip as it happens.

Pass your meal-list around on a clipboard, and ask volunteers to consider signing up for a meal (or two). Explain that a commitment means doing three things: fasting, giving the youth group a donation equal to the cost of a meal, and spending the designated time praying for the kids.

As a result, people will be praying and fasting on your behalf three times a day. If you're struggling during the trip, you'll know that people back home will be lifting you up in prayer.

This fund-raiser doesn't cost people anything because they'd have spent the money on food anyway. It's 100 percent profit, and the average donation is about $6.

Eric Johnson
Eau Claire, Wisconsin

TRY THIS ONE

1. ALPHABET SOUP

Stir up a pot of crazy excitement with this sloppy "soup" relay.

If you don't play this game outdoors, set out several drop cloths for easy cleanup. Form two teams, and set out two plastic kiddie pools at one end of the playing area. Fill the pools halfway with water, and add items that might make the pools look like giant bowls of soup, such as food coloring and plastic toy vegetables.

Write each of the letters of the alphabet on golf balls with a permanent marker. You'll need to add a full set of 26 golf balls to each pool of water (go to a golf course to buy cheaper used golf balls for this—maybe you can talk them into a donation). Then on "go" the first person on each team runs to a pool, jumps in with both feet, and looks for the letter A. Players have to retrieve the A golf balls with their toes, drop them over the side of the pool, and run back to their teams. The next player has to find the letter B, and so on. The winner is the first team to pull out all the golf balls in alphabetical order.

For a shorter version, you can use just vowels or number golf balls from one to 10.

Chad Kimberly
Janesville, Wisconsin

2. TISSUE SNATCHERS

Teenagers will have a "blast" with this fun and easy challenge!

Have your group form pairs, and give each pair a chair with a back, a drinking straw, a party favor (the type that uncurls when you blow in it), and 10 facial tissues.

Have one partner sit straddling the chair, facing its back, with the party favor in his or her mouth. Have the other partner lie on the floor face up, with his or her head at the feet of the other partner. The person on the floor will put a straw in his or her mouth, drape a facial tissue over the top of the straw, and blow the tissue up in the air. The partner in the chair then blows the party favor and tries to snatch the tissue with it.

The team that's captured the most tissues at the end of two minutes wins. See how many teams can finish without hyperventilating!

Bob Pankey
Whittington, Illinois

3. AUDIO SCAVENGER HUNT

Send teenagers on a wild hunt for noises around your church's grounds.

Separate your group into teams of three to five players each. Give each team a tape recorder, a blank tape, and a list of sounds they should record on the church grounds. Your list might include someone playing a piano, a toilet flushing, leaves crunching, crickets, a motorcycle revving, someone singing a TV theme song, someone mooing, someone answering the question, "What's your shoe size?" or someone answering the question, "Can you give driving directions to Ohio?" Tell players how much time they'll have, remind them of church rules, and begin the game. Award prizes to the team that comes back first within the time limit and to the team that finds the most recordings.

Our group thought it was a blast to listen to everyone's tape when teams returned!

Christina Rushing
Baltimore, Maryland

4. HUMAN FOOSBALL

Teenagers never had so much fun—staying put!

Use cones to set up two goals at opposite ends of a gym or open area. Add six masking-tape lines to your playing field, spaced apart equally, similar to the bars on a foosball table.

Form two teams, and have teams form groups of two or three. Have teammates sit on the playing field lines, alternating teams on each line, so that each team is scattered across the field like foosball players on a foosball field. Teams must face their opponent's goal. Provide a large beach ball, and tell players they must kick the ball into the goal in order to score. Players must sit on their lines. They cannot move and cannot touch the ball with their hands. Tell teams that they can lose points for unsportsmanlike conduct, such as putting down others, and they can gain points for sportsmanship, such as encouragement.

The first team that scores 10 goals wins!

Tera Colbert
Fountain Valley, California

5. FISH IN A BARREL

Here's a great summer game—just make sure kids know they're going to get wet!

Form a circular playing area about 30 feet in diameter with rope, cones, rocks, or anything else you have handy. This area will be the "barrel." Next mark off "fishbowls" inside the barrel, making each fishbowl about the size of a large Hula Hoop. You'll need one fishbowl for every four teenagers.

Have teenagers form two teams, and then have kids pair up within their teams. To begin, choose one team to take up positions inside the barrel—one person from each pair steps into one of the fishbowls and stays there, while his or her partner is free to move around inside the barrel area.

The other team's players are armed with water balloons, and all these players take up positions outside the barrel area. Their goal is to eliminate all the players inside the fishbowls by breaking water balloons on them. The inside team's goal is to have as many "fish" left as possible when a designated number of water balloons are thrown.

Whenever a water balloon breaks on a "fish" in a bowl, that person and his or her partner are out of play and must sit down. To avoid being hit, the "fish" in the bowls can dodge balloons, or their partners can block the balloons. These "free fish" can each take an unlimited number of hits. At the end of the round, award the inside team one point for every "fish" left in the fishbowls, and then have teams swap places.

Jon Sutton
DuBois, Pennsylvania

6. WINTER ICEBREAKERS

Teenagers will love playing winter-theme games...in a warm gym!

Choose any or all of these "cool" games for indoor wintertime fun. You can organize a tournament or use the ideas as opening icebreakers for your winter Sunday school sessions.

Ice Cube Hockey—Form two teams and ask players to stand around a smooth-surface table. Place plastic tubs as goals at either end of the table, assigning each team a goal. Then give each player a plastic spoon to use as a hockey stick. Substitute an ice cube for the puck, and have players try to score by swatting the ice cube with their spoons.

No-Snow Cones—Use paper snow-cone holders or roll paper into cones, and give each person a cone. Have students form pairs, and give pairs ice cubes to toss and catch in their cones. Make sure pairs move apart a few feet each time they catch their cube.

Shooting "Ice Stars"—Have students form two teams. Place two buckets as goals, and have teams stand back a few feet from the goals. Give each player an ice cube, and tell him or her to hold the cube for a few seconds so that it starts to melt. Then tell players to shoot for the goals by squeezing their cubes tightly to make them slide out of their hands.

Mary J. Davis
Marshalltown, Iowa

7. BOWLING BOGGLE

Plastic bottles with letters will give your group crazy bowling fun.

This bowling game takes a good amount of prep time, but it's worth it! You'll need 20 to 30 empty plastic soda bottles of the same size, but the larger, the better. You'll also need an old bowling ball, self-stick labels, a permanent marker, and water. Plan to play this game in a large, paved outdoor space such as a church parking lot—away from parked cars.

Wash the bottles and remove the labels. Write a letter of the alphabet on each self-stick label, and stick one label on each bottle. You don't need to make a label for each letter of the alphabet, but you should make several labels for each of the more common letters such as S, T, R, N, and vowels. Fill the bottles about one quarter full with water.

Configure the bottles in a traditional bowling triangle or in rows. Form teams, and have the teams stand behind a line about 30 to 40 feet away. Give each player two turns to bowl, and have players collect all the "pins" they knock down. After a certain time, or after everyone bowls, give teams two minutes to form words with the letters they have on their bottles. The team that forms the most words wins!

Kate Mattson
Woodbury, New Jersey

8. AFFIRMATION RELAY

Use a new twist on the relay race to encourage affirmations.

Form teams of about six people, and have each team stand in a line. Then have each team choose a leader to stand about 10 feet away from his or her team. Give each team leader a cup with slips of paper in it. Make sure that there are as many affirmations as there are team members. You might write these suggestions:

- Run to your youth leader and yell, "God loves you!"
- Run up to someone who's not on your team and give him or her a hug.
- Tell a member of the opposite sex an encouraging Bible verse.
- Give each team member a pat on the back and say, "Good job!"
- High five six people.
- Compliment someone on his or her shirt.
- Sing "Jesus Loves Me" to someone, and substitute *you* for *me* throughout.

Start the relay by allowing the first person in each line to run up to his or her team leader, grab an affirmation, complete the suggestion, and run back to the team, tagging the next person in line. The first team to complete all tasks is the winner.

Rebecca Kerr
Athens, Georgia

9. INDOOR BLIND CROQUET

Does your youth group have the winter blahs? Dig out that croquet set, and bring summertime fun inside!

Anchor the wickets in squares of craft foam, and set up the game in a traditional pattern in your fellowship hall. Or use the whole building to create a course that's more like miniature golf, incorporating "creative" obstacles! You might push chairs together to form arches, use extra-large mailing tubes for tunnels, or stack books in the middle of the course as hazards. (You'll need several croquet sets if you have a large group.)

Have teenagers form pairs, and give each pair a blindfold. One partner must wear the blindfold, and only this person may hit the ball. The other partner gives instructions but can't touch the mallet or the ball.

The winning team is the pair that completes the course in the fewest number of strokes.

Steve Case
Oviedo, Florida

10. WEAR OR DARE

Teenagers will love this grab-bag version of Truth or Dare.

Before your meeting, collect lots of old clothes—including menswear and women's clothing, shoes, glasses, formal wear, and nightgowns—from congregation members. Place the clothes in a large bag. You'll also need a die and some cards that have dares or challenges on them.

Have teenagers sit in a circle, and ask one person to roll a die. If the person rolls an odd number, he or she has to reach into the clothes bag, pull out the first item that's touched, and put it on. If the person rolls an even number, he or she selects a dare card and should do that dare. You can use the dare cards from a Truth or Dare board game, or you can make up your own dares, such as "Run outside and scream, 'Our youth group rocks!'" or "Have another person in your group pour a pitcher of water on your head."

Have the next person in the circle roll the die, and continue the game as long as you want. (The longer you play, though, the funnier it gets.) For a variation, play Hot Potato, letting whoever ends up with the potato roll the die.

Becky Karas
Lyons, Kansas

11. HERDING CATS

(Especially good for junior highers)

Junior highers become cat wranglers in this high-energy game.

For this game, you'll need to set up a racetrack in a long hallway that has one or two turns. Each player will need a foam pool noodle and several balloons.

Have your group form three or four teams of wranglers. Assign each team a balloon color, and have teams inflate three balloons for each person. Give wranglers pool noodles, and have them all line up at the starting line. Tell teams that the balloons are cats, and each team needs to herd its cats to the stockyards. Cats can't be touched or kicked—they can only be guided by the pool noodle.

When you say "go," all teams herd at the same time and use the pool noodles to sweep the balloons through the racetrack. You can place obstacles throughout the track, such as strobe lights and fans for a "prairie storm" or scattered chairs as briar patches. Place a large tub on its side at the end of the track; the first team to herd all its cats into the tub wins.

Bill Hickory
Springfield, Missouri

12. MUSICAL MADNESS

(Especially good for junior highers)

This noncompetitive version of Musical Chairs will keep your junior highers in stitches!

Make a circle of chairs, with one chair for every person. Randomly select some of the chairs and place signs on them with silly directions, such as "Sing 'Happy Birthday' in a duck voice," "Do jumping jacks while you sing a commercial jingle," "Shout as loud as you can for 30 seconds," and "Shake hands with everyone around you."

Play Musical Chairs as you normally would, allowing kids to walk around the circle of chairs as you play music. When you stop the music, everyone must sit, and those who land in chairs with instructions must perform the tasks.

Allow 30 to 60 seconds for kids to carry out the instructions, and then begin the music again.

Marie Gallo-Lethcoe
Daytona Beach, Florida

13. GIANT T-BALL

Build trust in your group by taking T-ball to "another level."

For this game, you'll substitute a beach ball and a tennis racket for the ball and bat. You'll also need bandannas and a 6-foot-long 2x4—attached at the bottom to a stable base, with a plastic bowl for a "tee" screwed to the top.

First have your group form two teams. The rules of the game are the same as regular baseball: two teams, three strikes, three outs—but the players pick partners and play in pairs with these "twists."

When a team is playing the outfield and infield, they guard the positions as pairs—each partner has one leg tied to the other person, and one of the partners is blindfolded.

The team at bat also plays in pairs—with one partner on the other person's shoulders. When the ball's in play, the batter-pair runs the bases in this "two-tiered" fashion.

Tanya Steeves
Moncton, New Brunswick

14. BIG TIME PING-PONG

Maybe you've given kids fun variations on other games by up-sizing the playing ball—but have you ever tried it with Ping-Pong?

You'll need four Ping-Pong paddles; two chairs; a Ping-Pong net; and one bouncy, oversized ball. Set the chairs in the middle of the playing area, far enough apart so that you can stretch the net out and attach each end to one of the chairs.

Play in pairs just as in ordinary Ping-Pong. (Make sure kids hold the paddles with both hands to avoid sore wrists.) Each winning pair then takes on a new set of challengers until everyone has played.

My teenagers love this game, and it's a great way to lead into a discussion on teamwork.

Tanya Steeves
Moncton, New Brunswick

15. ONE-ON-ONE "BROOMBALL"

All you need are two brooms, a ball, two goals...then just add fun!

Have your group form two teams, and give each team a broom. Place the ball in the center of your playing area, and ask each team to line up against opposite walls near the goals. Have team members each put one hand on the wall, and have one player hold the broom. Then have teams number off, so that each team member is assigned a number.

To begin play, call out a number. The two people assigned that number will each grab a broom and run to the ball to play against each other and try to score. These two opponents will continue playing until you call out another number; then they'll drop their brooms and allow the two people assigned to the new number to run to the brooms and continue playing.

If a player scores, team members will return to their team's wall to wait until another number is called.

The greatest battles are between girls and guys!

Mark Tucker
Toledo, Ohio

16. GROUP KICKBALL BLAST

Use this version of Kickball to help your large group "blow off steam"!

Set up three bases and a home plate. Each base should measure 5x5 feet. Form two teams of about 10 to 15 players. Choose one team to take the field. Have the kicking team divide into "player" groups of three to five members. Each team should have several player groups.

Each player group takes a turn at kicking (however they choose to) while holding hands together. Then that player group will round the bases (still holding hands). If a player group fails to keep holding hands while rounding the bases, it's called out. The regular rules for Kickball apply—catching a kicked ball is out, and players can be tagged on the legs or thrown out with the ball.

Paul Baldwin
Mishawaka, Indiana

17. LAST GEORGE STANDING

Here's a simple game you can start at a moment's notice and play with any size group.

You'll need a quarter for each player. Give teenagers inexpensive nail polish, and have them paint their initials on their quarters. Use masking tape to create a circle on a tile or wood floor. Then have kids kneel around the outside of the circle. Tell kids that when you say "go" they should all spin their coins into the middle of the circle. (Some of the coins will bounce off each other; others may end up spinning outside the circle.)

The winner is the one whose quarter is still spinning inside the circle after all others have stopped.

Steve Case
Oviedo, Florida

18. THE FLASH

(Especially good for junior highers)

Strobe lights add a novel element to this game for junior highers.

Form two teams, place them at opposite ends of the gym, and have each team choose two "guards." Give each team a basket filled with beanbags (you can also use small plastic balls or rolled-up socks). The baskets stay at "home base."

The teams' challenge is to get their beanbags into their "goals," which are buckets placed across the gym from their starting positions. For each goal, set up two floor mats and put the bucket in the middle. Leave room around the floor mats so the players can approach the goal from all sides.

Players can only take one beanbag at a time from their team's basket. They can't step on the mats to shoot or to retrieve "misses." The guards stand on the floor mats and attempt to block the other team's shots. Turn out the lights and turn on the strobe light to begin play. The team with the most points when one team is out of beanbags wins.

You can form more than two groups if you have a lot of players and play this as a round-robin event, with winners defending their championship against new teams.

Dave Kwapisz
Brantford, Ontario

19. PRISON DODGE BALL

Add a "prison" for more fun with this combination of Dodge Ball and Elimination.

Use two small foam balls and play this game using the rules of Dodge Ball, with the following exceptions:

(1) there are no teams,

(2) whenever a player picks up a ball, he or she has a pivot foot and must leave one foot in place while in possession of the ball, and

(3) a ring of chairs in the center of the room serves as a "prison."

Make sure you have one less chair than you have players. A player must go to prison if...

(1) hit by a ball,

(2) another player catches a ball he or she has thrown,

(3) the player runs while holding a ball, or

(4) a player runs through the jail.

A player who's in prison can be "freed" to play again if he or she catches a stray ball and is able to hit an active player with that ball. Also, players who have a ball in possession when they're sent to prison may take that ball into prison with them. Tell players they can be removed from the game for unnecessary roughness.

Anthony Nieuwsma
Grinnell, Iowa

20. FOUR-WAY, FOOD-FIGHT FLOOR HOCKEY

Turn ordinary floor hockey into silly, high-energy action by replacing pucks with plastic food toys!

For this game you'll need a hockey stick or broom for each player, four floor hockey goals, and four food-shaped toys—each shaped like a different food (for example, a hot dog, a hamburger, a steak, and a chicken leg). You can search pet stores or dollar stores for inexpensive food toys.

Form four teams, give each teenager a hockey stick, and have each team choose a goalie. Place a floor hockey net in the corners of your playing area (or use masking tape to make a 5x5-foot square on each wall), and assign each team a goal to defend. Place the four plastic toys in the middle of the playing area to start the game. Use the regular rules for floor hockey.

This game is great for leveling out the playing field. To raise the competition level, designate different point values to each of the plastic toys.

Rob Perrin
Calgary, Alberta

21. TIRE BOWLING

Generate some great summer fun for small- and medium-size groups.

For this game, you'll need 10 two-liter bottles, sand or water, one old car tire, a dry-erase board, and a few pairs of gloves.

Fill the bottles one-quarter full with sand or water to create bowling pins. Set up a triangle of pins in a parking lot or gym. Have a player put on a pair of gloves and "bowl" with the car tire. Allow each player to roll the tire only once in each frame for a total of five frames. Keep score on a dry-erase board; the player with the highest total wins!

Jeremy Andrews
Aurora, Illinois

22. PUZZLE BUSTERS

Use puzzles as the key ingredient in a fun and inexpensive group builder.

During one youth retreat, our kids fell in love with puzzles, so we added excitement by turning puzzle-making into a game.

You'll need three 250-piece puzzles and masking tape. Make a large tape square on the floor, and mix together the pieces of all three puzzles in the center of the square. Form three teams and have each team choose a place in the square to put a puzzle together. Assign each team a different puzzle to complete. Tell teams they have an hour to try and put their puzzles together. Any team caught hiding other teams' pieces will be penalized 10 puzzle pieces. The team with the most pieces put together after an hour wins.

Dustin Sauder
Manheim, Pennsylvania

23. GLOW BASKETBALL

Here's how to set up glow-in-the-dark basketball fun for your teenagers!

For this game, you'll need a glow-in-the-dark basketball (about $20), four glow-in-the-dark necklaces, and enough glow-in-the-dark bracelets for each group member to have one.

You'll need to purchase two colors of bracelets and necklaces to identify two different teams.

Form two teams, and give players their glow-in-the-dark bracelets. Use duct tape to attach two necklaces to each basketball hoop in your gym. Turn off the lights and play basketball with these additional rules: No rough play is allowed, and there's no out-of-bounds.

After the game, spend time talking about being a beacon of light in a dark world. Make sure to point out that the ball only glows in the dark after it has spent time in contact with a light source, and the bracelets only glow if they're broken so the chemicals can react. This corresponds to two spiritual truths: We can only reflect Jesus if we spend time with him, and our wills must be broken before we can be the light of Christ.

We used these Scripture verses for our discussion time: Matthew 5:14-16; Ephesians 5:8-10; Philippians 2:14-15; and 1 John 1:5-7.

Jennifer and Solano de Araujo
Bronson, Michigan

24. "WHAT'S IN THE BAG?" WORD SCRAMBLE

Use weird-feeling objects to spark a zany game.

You'll need one paper lunch bag for each player, tape, candy, and numerous "mystery objects" that feel weird to the touch, such as mushrooms, grapes, cooked noodles, dog biscuits, modeling dough, and marshmallows.

Before the meeting, you'll need to choose one funny or trendy phrase for each group of players. (The number of letters in each phrase should equal the number of players in each group.) Write one letter of the phrase on a paper bag, and assign each letter a consecutive number. So, for example, for the phrase "SpongeBob SquarePants," you would make a bag that has S-1, another bag that has P-2, another bag that has O-3, and so on. Fill each bag associated with one phrase with one of the mystery ingredients, then fold down the tops of the bags and tape them shut.

When teenagers arrive, give them each a bag and tell them they can't open their bags or tell anyone else what they think might be inside. Tell everyone that the goal of the game is to find the others who have the same mystery object—by feeling the contents of the bags—and then form a group. Then each group must figure out what its phrase is. The first team that correctly identifies its mystery object and phrase wins.

To add a level of challenge, don't add the numbers to the bags, and have teams try to de-scramble their word phrases.

Rebecca Reynolds
Kingsport, Tennessee

25. RANDOM DISC-GOLF FUN

Easy setup and scoring turn this game into quick Disc-Golf fun!

You'll need one flying disc for each player in this game, which can be played in any location with open space. Determine the number of holes prior to starting, based on how much time you have to play.

Select a player to go first, and allow that player to select a "flag": essentially anything in sight that's not a hazardous target—a tree, shrub, telephone pole, or playground equipment, for example. Each player then attempts to throw the disc to that flag and tracks his or her number of throws. As in regular Disc Golf, each person must throw his or her disc from where it lands. A flag is considered "holed" if any part of the disc touches the flag. Players can move their discs six feet in any direction from where they land, but players must take a stroke in order to do so. The player with the best score for each round chooses the next flag, or you can rotate players to begin each round.

Dave Bostrom
Maplewood, Minnesota

TRY THIS ONE

GROUP BUILDERS

1. JELLY BEAN TIMES

Who knew that jelly beans could spark such interesting discussions with both junior and senior highers?

Before your meeting, buy jelly beans, and sort them so you have one of each color to give every teenager. The colors will represent these emotions: yellow/fear; red/embarrassment; green/envy; blue/sadness; purple/anger; black/loneliness; orange/happiness; pink/love; white/courage.

Give everyone their jelly beans. Begin by having one person choose a jelly bean and share in one minute or less an experience related to that jelly bean color. Then go around the circle and have everyone else share a story related to that emotion. (As leader, you may wish to start each new color experience by sharing your story first.) If a teenager chooses not to tell about an experience, he or she can give that colored jelly bean to another person, and that person must share two experiences.

This activity encourages listening and sharing from the heart, and it strengthens emotional ties among the participants.

Lynne Turner
London, Ontario

2. VIDEO CAROLS

Turn Christmas caroling into team-building fun!

Hold this fun activity on a clear night during the Christmas season. Ask your congregation or youth group parents to lend you video cameras for the evening. Have your group form teams of six or less, and give each team a video camera. Tell teams they have 30 minutes to drive around neighborhoods and record as many Christmas carols on tape as they can. The trick is that they must videotape their teams singing the carols in front of Christmas decorations that are appropriate for the songs. For example, they might look for an illuminated crèche and sing "Silent Night" in front of it. They must use a different house for each Christmas carol they record. After the time limit, teams can reconvene at their meeting place and show the videos.

Larry Biel
Omaha, Nebraska

3. SENIOR-YEAR SCRAPBOOK

Create a memorable memento for each of your graduates with this "scrappy" idea.

Start in September to prepare meaningful graduation gifts for your group's seniors. Take lots of snapshots of the prospective graduates throughout the year. On each snapshot, record the senior's name, date, place, and activity. Then, as graduation nears, compile an individual scrapbook for each graduate.

This can be a time-consuming process, but it's one graduation gift that won't be forgotten.

David Reinhard
Muscle Shoals, Alabama

4. VALENTINE VIDEOS

Celebrate Valentine's Day by sending kids out with video cameras to document your church's great married couples.

Have teenagers form two teams, and give each team a video camera. Tell them they have one hour to videotape couples from the church singing love songs, reading poems to their spouses, or talking about how they first met and fell in love. Tell teams you'll award points for each person they videotape. You might award extra points for men because they're liable to be more reluctant. You might also provide teams with a list of addresses for church members. (Be sure to start this activity early enough in the evening. Even at 7 p.m. we caught people in their pajamas.) At the end of the hour, gather to watch the videos. If your church is planning a valentine dinner for couples, show the video at the dinner. Our group had a really fun time interacting with the adults, especially when we captured people on videotape whom we never imagined would sing for us!

Tina McGoogan
Junction City, Arkansas

5. AFFIRMATION STOCKINGS

Use the holiday season to encourage a spirit of affirmation among youth group members.

Several weeks before Christmas, give each student a white sock and set out items to decorate it, such as markers, fabric paint, glue, glitter, beads, stickers, and felt. Be sure students include their names on their socks as they decorate them.

When everyone is finished, hang the stockings in your meeting room or hallway for the month of December. Each time teenagers come to a meeting, they must write affirmations for at least two or three people. Or they can bring goodies to stuff in people's stockings. Encourage pastors and church members to visit the stockings and add affirmations. The week before Christmas, pass out the stockings for an uplifting Christmas gift.

Heather McMillan
Gladstone, Michigan

6. DOLLAR DAYS

One dollar can go a long way to help your teenagers reflect on their connection with God.

Take your teenagers to a mall, dollar store, or department store, and give them each a dollar. Tell them they must buy something for a dollar or less that describes God to them. Make sure they know they'll have to explain their purchase. If some kids are having a hard time finding something, you can suggest purchases such as a Hot Wheels car because God steers us in the right direction; an extra-large candy bar because there's more than enough of God to share and to give away; or water because God's Word hydrates us when the world dehydrates us. After 15-20 minutes, bring teenagers together to explain their purchases.

Use this activity again and again with different questions to help teenagers think about their relationship with God and others. Try these other dollar-day challenges: Purchase something that describes...

(1) what God has done for you,

(2) how Jesus helps you through difficult times,

(3) your gratitude to God,

(4) how you feel about sharing your faith, or

(5) what you love about your parents.

James Hill
Camas, Washington

7. MASK MAKING

Because of the intimate nature of this trust-building activity, it may work best with a group of kids who know each other well.

As an icebreaker, pair kids randomly, and have them share with their partners 10 different "favorites," such as a favorite sports team or radio station. Then have kids write each other's prayer requests on a piece of paper and save it for later.

Next distribute the mask-making supplies: 10-inch strips of plaster gauze (available from Dick Blick Art Materials, by calling 1-800-828-4548 or visiting their Web site at www.dickblick.com for a free catalog), bowls of water, towels, and ¼ cup of petroleum jelly for each pair. Have kids make the masks using the following process:

1. Have one partner lie on the floor.

2. Have the other partner apply the petroleum jelly to his or her partner's face.

3. Next instruct kids to dip the gauze strips into the water and carefully place them on their partner's face. Have them layer the strips, forming a mask, though the eyes and nose shouldn't be covered.

4. Allow approximately 20 minutes for the masks to dry, then have unmasked partners remove them carefully. During the 20-minute waiting period, have teenagers pray for their "masked" partners.

Have kids repeat the process with the other partner.

Once the masks are completed, have kids decorate them. Afterward use the masks to decorate your youth room.

Marilyn Nash
Chicago, Illinois

8. BIBLE BUBBLES

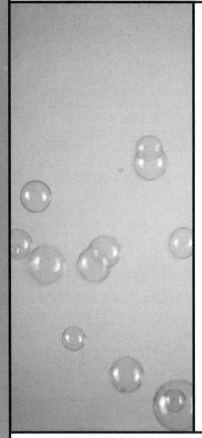

The big bubble created in this activity helps kids see the application of Romans 15:5-6, "May the God who gives endurance and encouragement give you a spirit of unity among yourselves as you follow Christ Jesus, so that with one heart and mouth you may glorify the God and Father of our Lord Jesus Christ."

You'll need liquid bubbles, a bubble wand for each group member, and a Bible.

Have kids blow bubbles on their own for a few minutes. Then have everyone gather, and explain the idea to them.

Have one person blow a bubble and catch it on his wand. Then a second person dips her wand and places it carefully on the first bubble. She then blows a second bubble attached to the first. (Both wands remain in place.) A third bubble is blown onto the two by another person, and so on. All wands remain attached to the larger, complex bubble. Cooperation is needed to support the bubble from different angles and to aid in distribution of the liquid bubbles. If one member blows too hard or disrupts the wands, the bubble breaks free or pops.

Read Romans 15:5-6. Ask:

- What kind of bubble were we able to build together?
- How is that different from or similar to the kind of bubble we could build alone?
- Why is it important for Christians to glorify God with one heart and mouth?

Close your time together in song, glorifying God.

Catherine Elliott
Rockledge, Florida

9. ISLAND ARRIVAL AND SURVIVOR

See how well your group members know each other.

Give each person an index card (or a sheet of paper) and a pencil. Have them each write their name on their card and number their card from 1 to 10.

Next to each number, have kids write the following:

1 to 5: List five things you'd take with you if stranded on a desert island for a year.

6: If someone were washed up on shore, who would you like it to be?

7: A care package washes ashore. Would you want it to be a pizza, a gallon of ice cream, or a dozen doughnuts?

8: During the night, you hear strange sounds. Which would scare you the most: a large, wild, hungry boar; your little brother who arrived on the island and is making those annoying noises; or the only possible rescue boat leaving the island?

9: Halfway through your yearlong adventure, your youth leader comes to visit. What does he or she say to you?

10: You find out Hollywood is going to make a movie about your adventure. Who would act your part?

Collect all the index cards. Read each card, and have kids guess whose card each one is. If you have more than 10 kids, read numbers 6 through 10 only from each card.

Darryl Duer
Ocean City, New Jersey

10. MAKE A MEMORY NIGHT

Here's a can't-miss community builder for youth groups of all ages.

You'll need groups of no more than 10 kids and one van for each group. You'll also need adults who don't mind having some silly fun with the kids.

Begin by gathering all the kids into one room. One at a time, lead them into a second room. Ask the first young person to name any local location (for example, a city park). Lead in a second young person, and ask him or her to name any kind of silly activity (for example, playing Leapfrog). You now have your first "activity": playing Leapfrog at the park. Continue, without revealing what's going on, until you have five activities for each group. Then send the groups out to their locations, and have them document their assigned activities with Polaroid photos. This leads to some really crazy time spent together! Afterward have all the groups return to share their photos with each other.

Eric Gerken
St. Petersburg, Florida

11. GROUP DIVIDERS

If your group-forming ideas are tired, wake them up with these fresh twists.

Have everyone draw a colored slip of paper out of a hat. Everyone with the same color is on the same team. This is a great way to divide a large group into pairs. Chuckle as you watch an 11th-grade wrestler wave a small pink slip of paper in the air as he tries to find his partner.

Or divide your group using drawings or illustrations. For example, illustrate half the slips of paper with a picture of fish and the other half with a picture of a doctor wearing a mask. After kids have found others with the same pictures, they must figure out their group's name. Tell kids the names of the groups match the pictures and they rhyme. For example: Surgeons vs. Sturgeons or Hogs vs. Dogs. For added humor, draw the pictures yourself.

Tracey Westphal
Wyoming, Michigan

12. WORLD'S GREATEST INVENTION

Here's an inventive way to beef up kids' creativity.

A week ahead of time, invite kids to bring their best ideas to a World's Greatest Invention Party. Make it an all-day affair. Spend the week gathering as much "stuff" as possible, such as appliance boxes, used poster board, hub caps, bicycle parts, broken small appliances, rope, tape, aluminum foil, markers, paint...anything!

When kids arrive, have them form teams of no more than four. Have each team draw plans for its invention on a sheet of newsprint. Tell kids their invention doesn't have to be functional, just creative. Suggest things like time machines or space capsules.

After kids draw their plans, turn them loose to build their inventions. Give them plenty of time. And feed them well; inventing is hard work.

For added fun, videotape the progress of each invention. Or take photographs to be published in the local newspaper or youth group newsletter.

Award prizes for the most creative invention, the ugliest invention, the most useless invention, and the biggest invention.

Mark Simone
Ravenna, Ohio

13. RETREAT EATS

Due to lack of room in a crowded van, I let kids attending a retreat shop for the meals.

I divide kids into "grub teams" and assign them a meal or two, depending on the number of attendees. I then give teams a budget, the number of people they must feed, and reminders that they need to get all the necessary ingredients to make fairly balanced meals. Then I let them loose in a supermarket close to our retreat destination (always making sure beforehand that there is one!).

I buy supplies such as dish soap and paper products, and I help kids with logistics. For example, I'll ask, "How are you going to cook frozen pizzas for 20 people with one oven?" or "Maybe you should reconsider how many others like Spam." The grub teams also cook the meal they shop for (with adult supervision), and another team cleans up.

This is a terrific way to get kids to interact with people they may not have connected with otherwise. It helps break the ice at the beginning of a retreat, gives kids ownership, and keeps retreat costs down. And the food the kids cook has always been much better and more creative than "camp food." My youth group now complains if they don't get to do this.

Nicole Smith
Dunedin, Florida

14. BIBLE STORY SIMULATORS

No one loses in these games, because everyone wins when kids help each other. Create these situations for your youth group to learn even more about working together.

• Crossing the Red Sea—Designate two boundaries about 8 feet apart. Place a sheet of paper in the center of the gap to serve as a stone that kids may stand on. Have your group work together to get everyone across the gap, without anyone falling in.

• Escaping the Lions' Den—Form a circle of chairs around your group. Set a time limit of 30 seconds for each person. If you have six kids, you'd allow three minutes. Tell the group to work out a plan to get everyone out of the "den" before the lions are released or the time is up. No one may touch a chair.

• Climbing Jacob's Ladder—Designate a 1-foot-wide straight area on the floor. Have your group members stand in a straight line in that area. Then have the group work out a way to reverse their order without stepping out of the 1-foot boundary. (The team will be moving back and forth like the angels did on Jacob's ladder.)

Jimmie Small
Denville, New Jersey

15. WHAT A TRIP!

Send your group on a pseudo-vacation with just a camera and some creativity!

For this adventuresome afternoon, assign groups of kids to specific vehicles. Give each vehicle a local road map, a camera, one roll of film, and these instructions:

Your mission is to take photos of your group that create the illusion you're on a vacation together. Creatively take pictures that represent places, transportation, and activities. You'll get one point for each picture you take of your group on vacation and one bonus point for each picture that no other group takes. Remember to respect businesses, be as non-disruptive as possible, and ask permission when appropriate.

Give kids a designated time to meet at a one-hour photo lab, drop off their film, and then meet at church for supper. Pick up the pictures one hour later, and give each group a sheet of neon poster board to create a vacation display.

Our kids posed on horses, in boats, on motorcycles, at airports, by race cars, and on a caboose. They took pictures at hotel swimming pools, in ethnic restaurants, and in western-wear stores. Using their maps, kids found towns within a 30-mile radius named Miami, Nevada, Mexico, Peru, Russiaville, New London, and Bunker Hill. They also posed by street signs with names of vacation spots, such as Washington, Orleans, and Colorado.

We put all the vacation displays in the fellowship hall so church members could enjoy the kids' creative destinations.

Kevin Niles
Hemlock, Indiana

16. WHERE ARE YOUR LEADERS COMING FROM?

When our youth group attendance dropped after we lost our adult volunteers, we recruited new leaders and decided to introduce our kids to them in an unusual way. Try it, and watch your kids get as excited about coming to youth group as our kids are.

Form as many teams as you have adult leaders. Give each team a set of clues—serious and silly—each regarding the identity of a different leader. For example, clues could include: This person was caught painting the high school lawn red, has brown hair, is an accomplished puzzle-builder, craves pistachio nuts, and reads comic books in bed.

Have the leaders stay in their homes with prepared refreshments and personal mementos, such as scrapbooks, trophies, or handmade crafts. Instruct teams to read their set of clues and go to the house of the person who fits those clues. If the guess is wrong, the team must try again. If the team guesses correctly, the team members may stay at that house, enjoy the refreshments, and learn more about that leader.

After one hour, have teams and leaders gather at your house for games and more food. Use crowdbreakers and games that'll help kids and leaders get to know each other better.

Sylvia Montefu
Plant City, Florida

17. ONE BODY

Help teenagers understand the biblical concept of unity with this group builder.

Use a photocopier to make your youth group into one body! Assign each teenager one body part—left ear, right ear, left eye, right eye, left arm, right arm, and so on. (Students who are the "eyes" should be instructed to keep their eyes closed while photocopying.) As students are photocopying their designated part, work to place the photocopies together to assemble your group's "body."

After your body is assembled, remove one of the arms and proclaim that it is not needed. Read 1 Corinthians 12:14-27, and then reattach the arm. Discuss these questions with your group:

- What was it like to watch a body part being removed?
- How is the arm different now that it is reattached? How is it the same?
- What's it like when you feel left out of a group?
- How do you share your gifts with this group?

Keep your "body" on display as a reminder to your group of how Christ wants us to function together.

Leslie Bogar
Littleton, Colorado

18. FRIENDSHIP STONE

"Cement" real friendships in your youth group by building stepping stones together!

For our group of nine students, we used two 60-pound bags of cement, one 14-inch plastic plant saucer for each group member, a garden hose, a wheelbarrow, and cooking spray. Ask students to bring decorative items to add to their stepping stones, such as marbles, plastic craft gems, LEGOS, old jewelry or key chains, decorative rocks, pennies with the minted dates of their birth years, and tile or ceramic pieces. Tell them they'll need items for their own stone as well as one item for each group member's stone.

Mix the cement in the wheelbarrow according to instructions, using the garden hose to add water. Have kids spray their plant-saucer "molds" with cooking spray, and pour the cement into the molds. Have each student design his or her stone by including decorative items, handprints, images drawn with a pencil tip, and the day's date. Then have kids contribute one decorative item to each other person's stone. When your group is done, everyone's stepping stone should include an item from every person in the group.

You can also use the instructions on the About.com Web site (http://familycrafts.about.com/cs/steppingstones) to choose what stepping stone project is right for your group size and ability.

Barbara Lam
Ellicott City, Maryland

TRY THIS ONE

HELPFUL HINTS

I WAS AT THE POLE

1. SCRIPTURE BOXES

Use this idea with small groups to help kids create and keep Scripture-fueled answers at their fingertips.

For each young person, we purchased an index-card box, multicolored index cards, alphabetical index-card dividers, and paint markers (available at most hobby stores). Kids decorated their Scripture boxes; then each one thought of subjects they'd like to learn more about from God's Word. Our group came up with more than 25 topics, including "anger" and "temptation." Every other week groups looked for 5 to 10 Scripture passages related to a particular topic, wrote the references on index cards, and filed them in the Scripture boxes alphabetically by topic.

This is a great tool for teenagers to use on a daily basis, no matter where they are or what challenges they face.

Karen Looney
Greensboro, North Carolina

2. ENCOURAGEMENT CHAIR

Take a short time each week to build unity and self-esteem in your teenagers.

Each week after everyone's arrived and you've made announcements, ask one teenager to sit in the "encouragement chair" (you can pick a more cutting-edge or silly term if you prefer). Ask the group to take turns giving compliments and sharing memories about that person. Be sure all the comments are positive. The volunteer may be slightly embarrassed at first, but most teenagers will be surprised and touched by what their peers say. Ask a different person to sit in the encouragement chair each week. With a small youth group, this may be a six- to 12-week activity, but with a large youth group, you may be able to do this for months.

Schuyler Peterson
Georgetown, South Carolina

3. WHERE IN THE WORLD ARE YOU? SAN DIEGO?

Keep track of group members and their families during the summer with this idea. It'll remind kids that you're still a church family even when you're apart.

Post a large map of the United States on a bulletin board. When group members' families go on vacation, have them send postcards to your office. Then photocopy the note part of the postcard and put it up on the bulletin board next to the picture side of the postcard. Fasten a colored string from the vacation location to your church city with pushpins.

Jill Capper
Crawfordsville, Indiana

TRY THIS ONE

4. TIE A YELLOW RIBBON...

Here's a great idea to help your traveling party stand out in the crowd!

Next time your youth group hits the airport for a missions trip or retreat, tie a brightly colored ribbon around each piece of luggage that belongs to your group. Then in baggage claim, instead of trying to read luggage tags as bags go flying by on the conveyor belt or watching teenagers fight with crowds to grab their luggage, simply spot the ribbons and pull the bags aside in a pile for your group. Be sure to tally the number of bags beforehand so you can just count the bags as you pull them off.

Drew Moser
Upland, Indiana

5. SEXUAL PURITY

Give girls a special treat to reinforce a message about maintaining sexual purity.

After a discussion with our youth group on sexual purity, we asked the girls to reserve a half-day on Saturday to be pampered! We told them to fix their hair but not to wear any makeup. When they arrived at the church, we gave each of them a Mary Kay facial and makeup session. Then we took everyone to a local bridal shop where all the girls tried on wedding gowns so they could see how beautiful a pure bride looked and felt. (We made arrangements with the shop ahead of time.)

The girls had fun—but we could see the seriousness on their faces as they looked at themselves in the mirrors.

Mary Ann Carrasco
Odessa, Texas

6. CARTOON COMMUNICATION

Recycle the smiles from daily desk-calendar pages with this idea.

I used to throw away daily desk-calendar pages, but now I use them as stationery to write notes to my kids. You can write in the margin at the side or on the back of the page.

The daily pages are a great reminder to write one teenager or adult volunteer each day, and this simple gesture lets kids and adults know I'm thinking about them and praying for them. Also, because I use pages from The Far Side calendar, it gives them a laugh at no extra cost!

Michael Wilson
Dyersburg, Tennessee

7. TRANSPARENT WORSHIP

Are you looking for a use for that old overhead? Here's how we used ours to create a memorable worship service.

Before the teenagers arrived, we cut transparency film into two-inch strips and set out a collection of different-colored overhead markers.

At the beginning of the worship service, we gave students a topic to think about—a characteristic of God that gives them comfort (any topic would work, though). Then we asked them each to write a word or phrase that represented their feelings. While we sang worship songs that tied in with our theme, we invited young people to come up and each place their strip on the overhead projector. The strips transformed the white screen into a multicolored banner glorifying God.

Walter Surdacki
Campbell, California

8. PROGRESSIVE CLUE HUNT

Send kids out into the neighborhoods in search of food...and laughs!

This fun activity combines two old favorites—a progressive dinner and a clue hunt. Before the event, ask some parents to prepare one of the meal courses at their home as a stop for the progressive dinner. Plan four stops for appetizers, soup or salad, a main course, and dessert. Then prepare rhymes that give clues to the four locations.

Separate the group into teams of four, making sure each team has a car and driver. You may want to ask for parental permission for this event because it includes travel. Give each team a set of clues and a map. Ask adult sponsors to drive, making sure they don't offer assistance in finding houses. You may provide the drivers with the actual address, in case time runs short and kids still haven't figured out clues. Be sure you don't put the clues in any order, so kids don't know what course they will be served when they find the house they're looking for.

Tell teams to meet after a certain time (or you may decide to have everyone meet for the dessert course last), so you can share fun, clue-hunting stories.

Tony Akers
Huntsville, Alabama

9. SENIOR CD

Take the time to collect memories for your seniors, and you'll be able to give them a great send-off.

If you and some of your youth group members have digital cameras, get into the habit of bringing those cameras to every single event, and take plenty of pictures! Even the smallest events can foster great photo opportunities that show the friendships your group members have made. Then, when a senior from your youth group graduates or is about to go off to college, together a photo CD for him or her.

Collect all the digital photos on your computer's hard drive, organizing and titling the photos by activity and year. Then copy them onto a CD—you may even make a scrapbook that complements the CD, so other group members can add notes and best wishes.

Mark Groen
Sandusky, Ohio

10. WEDDING VOWS

To address sexual purity with your students, invite their parents to help you!

Decorate the church sanctuary as if for a wedding. Have parents sit in the front pews, and then gather students at the back of the church or in the balcony. Ask students to describe what they'll expect from the person they'll marry someday. Ask them to describe what they'll give to that person in return (for example, love, trust, help, and so on). Remind students that God gives us all these things through his love. Describe God's plan for marriage and his warnings about sexual sin (Genesis 2:24; 1 Corinthians 6:12-20). Be sure to present this loudly and clearly enough so that parents can hear too.

Then tell students that they'll each have a few minutes at the altar with someone who loves them. Have wedding-themed music start, and send each teenager, one at a time, to meet his or her parents at the altar for a private moment. Parents can then share their hopes, prayers, and thoughts about sexual purity.

Provide a small gift such as a ring or a flower for each teenager as a reminder of the ceremony.

Dana Sears
Ocean View, Delaware

11. A POSTER FOR YOUR THOUGHTS

Use this idea for any retreat, trip, or mission experience that your kids are involved in. By doing so, you'll include your church in your kids' events and ensuing growth.

Throughout World Vision's 30-Hour Famine lock-in, we had our kids write their feelings, thoughts, and prayers on a piece of poster board. Then we displayed it at church for all to read. Some church members who hadn't sponsored the kids did so after reading the kids' comments.

Ten of our kids raised $2,150 through sponsorship, aided by the poster.

Wendy Weber
Colfax, Wisconsin

12. VERSE CHANTS

Help teenagers learn Scripture verses and have fun while they're doing it!

Our youth group does what we call verse chants at the end of each Sunday school class. Before class, I take our weekly verse and split it into four parts, writing each section on a separate piece of poster board. The class forms four groups, and each group goes to a corner of the room with one segment of the verse. Then they each decide on hand motions to illustrate their segment. For example, one group might point to the sky to represent God or hug themselves to represent love. After a few minutes, we round up the class. Then each group chants its part of the verse, along with the appropriate gestures. We recite the verse 10 to 15 times in a row.

It's amazing how quickly kids will learn Scripture verses when they're having fun doing it!

Beth Bishop
West Columbia, South Carolina

13. CHRISTIAN SURVIVAL BAG

Give your teenagers a tool that will help them through difficult times.

For every person in your group, put together a "Christian survival bag"—a sandwich bag that has in it a nail, a cross, a marker, a rock, a penny, and a candle (optional). Add to each bag a sheet of paper that explains what each item means:

• Nail—Jesus still feels the pain every time you sin.

• Cross—When in doubt, take the "cross road."

• Marker—God has a permanent mark upon your soul.

• Rock—Cast this rock upon the ground—instead of at others.

• Penny—You have the "cents" to know that Jesus loves you!

• Candle—Jesus is the light of the world.

Hand out the bags at the end of a retreat or service, and tell kids that when they are frustrated, overwhelmed, or stressed, they can reach for their survival bags.

Doreen Gerczak
Spring, Texas

14. YOUTH SHOWER

Use the concept of a bridal shower to help your kids feel like an important part of the church as a whole.

You've heard of baby showers and bridal showers—why not a youth shower? Send a letter to each committee in your church, asking for a small gift for your youth group. Suggest that the gift be something related to that committee's ministry. Ask each committee to include a card with the gift explaining the committee's purposes or activities, as well as ways that the youth group members might be able to offer their help. Then invite committee representatives to bring their gifts to the youth shower. As you enjoy snacks and games, let kids open the gifts.

Our youth shower turned into a ministry fair with a twist! We received wind chimes from the choir, a Monopoly game from the finance committee, and baked goods from the hospitality committee. Our kids were amazed at how our church operates, how it helps people, and how they fit in as a part of the church.

Mary Mattingly and Marlene Wukusick
Batesville, Indiana

15. PANTRY-SHELF PRAYER

Here's a great prayer idea you can do with your group members in a grocery store.

Take your group shopping, and ask each person to take a few minutes to find an item. Form small groups, and have group members work together to make up a prayer using each grocery item they've collected. They can use the brand name of the item or a word or phrase from the label. For example, one group might have a prayer like this: "Dear God, thank for the (Joy) you bring us. Help us to (Cleanser) hearts of sin and never be (Chicken) to follow you. We (Depends) on you like (Peas) in a pod!"

Give each group about five minutes to think of a prayer. Have groups present their prayers to the whole group, holding up each item as it appears in the prayer.

Consider gathering the items together and donating them (with the prayers written out and attached) as part of a local food drive.

Pete Clapsis
Zephyrhills, Florida

16. THIS LITTLE LIGHTHOUSE

These "little lights" will make great adult leader affirmations.

Purchase miniature lighthouses, or use small lights of any kind, such as Christmas tree lights, birthday candles, or key-chain flashlights. Attach a note similar to the following:

"When I saw this little lighthouse, I thought of you and our church's ministry to young people. There were bigger lighthouses I could've purchased, but I felt this represented us more—everyday folks caring for kids in some very everyday ways. Thank you for sharing your light with us. Together we're making a brighter way for our kids! Place this in a prominent place, somewhere you will see it each day, and think to yourself, 'I'm a light!' Keep shining for Jesus!"

Tony Akers
Bowling Green, Kentucky

17. NAME-A-HOLIDAY CHALLENGE

Here's something fun to try the next time you and your group are sitting around a table at a fast-food restaurant.

Have someone start by naming a known holiday, one found on a typical calendar. Then have each person take a turn naming a holiday. Be sure to remember religious holidays and historical celebrations. Keep going around the circle, until someone is stumped or repeats a holiday that's already been mentioned—that person gets to clean up the trash when your meal is over.

This is a great activity for long road trips, and it gets to be more fun as it's repeated. Resist the temptation to switch topics—this works best if you only use holidays every time you play. Note: Be sure you set your own limits. Sure, there may be a National Pretzel Day, but you aren't going to find that on the usual calendar. Don't discount holidays from other religions.

Windermere Union Youth Group
Windermere, Florida

18. GRADUATION GIFTS

These personalized gifts will make great keepsakes for all your graduating seniors.

Find a Scripture that says something about a graduating senior's personality or one that will offer personal encouragement or challenge. Using a nice font, create a page with the teenager's name at the top, followed by the selected verse, then your church's name and date at the bottom.

Kids love to have something personalized, and freshmen and sophomores look forward to seeing which verses you'll pick for them when they graduate.

Mike Ayers
Topeka, Kansas

19. SENSATIONAL SEATING

We've installed restaurant booths in our meeting room—they're an exciting addition and add a sense of cohesiveness to our room. Here's how we got them.

Instead of building booths, we let our fingers do the walking and called the business that owns the majority of the restaurants in our town. I asked if they had booths they'd be willing to part with as they remodeled or closed restaurants. They did and offered the booths to us for only $75 each!

Our group made the trek to Saginaw to avoid the extra delivery charge. The booths were heavy to move, but worth the effort. Better yet, a member of our congregation thought the project was worthwhile enough to spring for our travel expenses!

The booths work well as workstations, prayer stations, a convenient way to divide teams, or seating for a coffeehouse night. We placed "table tents" on each table to announce upcoming concerts and events, along with an empty Nehi soft drink bottle–our group's name–complete with a flower. We plan on adding tabletops personalized by our kids–probably lacquered collages–and we'll use checkered tablecloths for nicer occasions.

Corby Blem
Mt. Pleasant, Michigan

20. "SEE YOU AT THE POLE" STICKERS

This simple idea will encourage your teenagers to identify themselves as a part of the body of Christ.

Encourage your youth group to participate in See You at the Pole (www.syatp.org). The commitment and excitement of this event will get the attention of the most lethargic teenager. Then commemorate kids' enthusiasm with a visual reminder of their participation. Purchase self-sticking address labels from an office supply store and design a sticker. It might say, "I Was at the Pole" or "Did You See Me at the Pole?" As students return to their classes, hand out stickers for your teenagers to wear. They'll be great conversation starters at school, and your only problem will be having enough to go around!

Shad Purcell
Fair Oaks Ranch, Texas

21. FAMILY BUILDERS FOR THE HOLIDAYS

Thanksgiving, Christmas, and New Year's offer kids the most focused family time they'll experience all year. But for many families, the holidays are also very stressful times of the year.

Help your group members make the most of their family time by encouraging them to...

- —focus on people, not presents;
- —enjoy older relatives—play games with them, ask questions about their childhood holiday celebrations, and listen to their stories;
- —enjoy younger relatives—play games with them, take them places, and help them make gifts for others; and
- —help with chores and holiday preparations without being asked.

As youth leaders, we can help our kids spend quality time with their families by...

- —scaling back our programming during the holidays;
- —planning a fun event that involves families; and
- —encouraging them to serve their families.

Joanne Irwin
Lyons, Colorado

22. MINISTRY WISH LIST

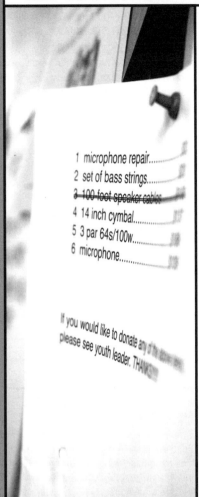

1 microphone repair.....
2 set of bass strings.....
3 100-foot speaker cables
4 14 inch cymbal.....
5 3 par 64s/100w.....
6 microphone.....

If you would like to donate any of the above, please see youth leader. THANKS!

This alternative to fund-raising will help you discover that God knows your needs and is able to touch the hearts of others to help you.

Instead of talking your congregation and community into buying another chocolate bar, doughnut, or auction item, try making a list of what your needs are and seeing if you can find benefactors! Be sure to keep your list focused on a specific project and explain what will be accomplished when your needs are met.

For example, if you'd like to raise money for your youth group's band, you might make a list like this one:

1 microphone repair $32

1 set of bass strings $20

2 microphone stands $64

2 100-foot speaker cables $100

1 microphone $109

1 14-inch cymbal $137

3 Par 64 lights/1000w $188

1 speaker $600

Have your group design the list, and then post it where most of your church members will see it, along with information about how to donate. Be sure to keep the list updated, crossing off items that people have helped you purchase. Your list will show church members that you have a plan of action, and they'll be able to see where their money goes. When you've checked off your list completely, celebrate with the donors in a way that shows that their generosity was put to good use. So, if you're asking for funds for your youth band, you can hold a celebration concert using your new equipment.

Chris Binion
Carrollton, Virginia

23. GAME NIGHT PRIZES

We use this idea as an incentive to get everyone to participate...and they do!

You'll need 100 letter-size envelopes, tickets or slips of paper, and the prizes.

Number the envelopes 1 to 100, and enclose a prize in each envelope. Tape the envelopes in order to a wall or chalkboard. Prizes could include small items such as bubble gum, three or four hard candies, sticks of chewing gum, school paraphernalia, coupons from fast-food restaurants, pencil sharpeners, magnets, or stickers. Fill one or two envelopes with a special prize, such as a $5 bill or a nice gift certificate. Don't forget to include "dud" prizes, such as a single playing card, a couple of tissues, an out-of-focus photograph, and so on.

Give the winner(s) of each round of each game a ticket with a number on it. The numbers correspond to the numbers on the envelopes. This random "luck of the draw" takes the pressure off of having "good" prizes. Also, your game night takes on the feel of a TV game show because kids choose the prizes sight unseen.

Joyce Ravnikar-Kulyk
Fairview, Pennsylvania

24. SHADOW-SCREEN NATIVITY

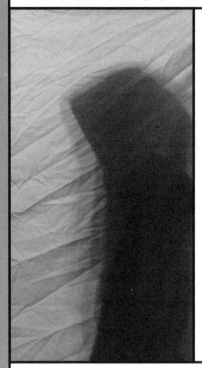

Celebrate this Christmas Eve with the holy family via shadow screen.

We take a king-size white sheet and lash it to a frame made of PVC pipe. Then we place this screen at the front of our worship space with an outdoor spotlight behind it. We recruit two teenagers to play Mary and Joseph. A manger full of straw is placed in the center behind the screen. We borrow a baby (four months or younger, if possible) from a church family and loosely wrap the baby in a blanket.

At the beginning of the service, the house lights are turned down low while the holy family takes their places behind the screen. Then the spot is turned on and the music begins. (I like "In the First Light" by Glad.) While the song plays, Mary and Joseph interact with the baby Jesus—holding him, cradling him, and passing him to each other. Near the end, Joseph unwraps the baby, carresses the feet, and counts the child's fingers. The shadow enlarges the characters and conveys an awe-inspiring vision of the divine yet human child being cared for by his earthly parents. (Hints: The Boy Scouts are a good group to make a manger or the shadow screen. And if the baby cries, all the better.)

Jacqui Ryan
Clatskanie, Oregon

25. PRAYER IDEAS

Kids will be more apt to pray for each other when they see you and your youth leaders modeling prayer with these ideas.

You'll need seven manila envelopes, each labeled with one day of the week. Post the manila envelopes in a prominent place in your meeting area. Divide up and write kids' names on the envelopes so you're praying for some group members each day. Then it's time for you and your adult leaders to start praying! If kids have specific prayer requests, they can jot them down and slip them into the appropriate envelopes.

Or purchase an address card file and write your kids' names and phone numbers on the cards. Each day, flip over a new card, praying for the person on the card. If time permits, give kids each a call on "their day," just to let them know you're praying for them and to ask for prayer requests. It's easy to add new names, and when you get all the way through the file, flip back to the beginning and start over!

Lisa Tweardy
Pittsburgh, Pennsylvania

Jayne Zirkel
Waco, Texas

26. WORDS TO LIVE BY

Bust the boredom on your youth group's next road trip with this thought-provoking activity.

Give teenagers the task of writing a "quote to live by"—a motto or statement that's inspiring or uplifting. This task should generate rewarding travel-time discussions, and teenagers will be amazed at their friends' intuitiveness.

Once you've reached your destination, have teenagers share their mottos, and award prizes for the funniest, the most inspiring, or the most generated by one vehicle.

Some of our group's best quotes were: "God's commandments are a perfect 10," "Being a pew potato leads to a half-baked spiritual life," "Dream big, do bigger," "Sometimes the best way to get someone to listen is to be quiet."

Melinda Sinn
Manhattan, Kansas

27. VALENTINE AFFIRMATION

Take your girls' focus off boyfriends this Valentine's Day, and turn it toward the true source of love.

Last January, as I talked to our group, I was shocked at how many girls hated Valentine's Day because—you guessed it—no boyfriend, no present. So I thought Valentine's Day would be a great opportunity to show our girls how much God (and our group) cared about them.

I contacted a member of our church (who happens to be a florist) and ordered a red rose for each girl in our group as well as any high school girl who had visited our church, Sunday school, or youth group. The rose was packaged attractively, nestled with some baby's breath in valentine paper. Then for each girl, we handmade a card with her name on the outside and a note inside. The roses were delivered to the high school the Friday before Valentine's Day.

We received lots of positive comments from the girls such as, "That's the first Valentine's present I ever received—your church must really love teenagers."

Richard Parker
Russellville, Alabama

TRY THIS ONE

OUTREACH

1. SECRET SERVANTS

Spice up an ordinary snow-shoveling project with a bit of colorful fun.

Shoveling driveways and walkways for seniors is always a great outreach project for teenagers, though it can wear out the most cheerful of heart. So add a fun twist to your project with colored water.

Before heading out to your sites, fill several water bottles with water tinted with various shades of food coloring. Once your group has finished shoveling snow, have teenagers write friendly messages in the snow, such as "This youth group loves you!" or "With Jesus' Love." If you shovel snow without the resident knowing, you can write, "The Secret Servants were here!" in the snow. The residents will appreciate the service and enjoy the bold message.

Michael Casey
Pittsburgh, Pennsylvania

2. LAMB MINISTRY

Teenagers can use a stuffed lamb to talk with curious onlookers about Christ.

Our youth group has used a stuffed lamb toy as an outreach and Scripture learning tool. Each week a different teenager must take the lamb and carry it wherever he or she goes. The lamb cannot be hidden or stored away in a backpack or locker. The teenager must be prepared to teach about Christ as the Lamb of God to those who ask and discuss what it means to be a Christian. After one week, another teenager may take ownership of the lamb. Our group has a constant waiting list of youth group members who want to carry the lamb.

For extra impact, give your lamb an acronym name such as ELLIE: Evangelizing Love and the Lord In Everything.

Dorothy Edwards
White Bear Lake, Minnesota

3. TAILGATE OUTREACH

Host this fun and inexpensive event during Super Bowl weekend—a tailgate party in your church parking lot!

Depending on the size of your group, circle a number of trucks, SUVs, and cars with hatchbacks. Use a truck bed as your staging platform for worship and teaching. Provide lots of food and time for fellowship.

Promote the event as an opportunity to invite friends—it gives kids a comfortable way to check out your youth ministry program.

If you plan this outreach before the Super Bowl or another sports event, be sure to make arrangements inside the church so you can all watch the game together.

Bryan Rogers
Midlothian, Texas

4. WEDNESDAY WHEELBARROWS

Here's a non-threatening way to take the love of Christ "outside the walls."

Every year or so, we take our teenagers out for a Wheelbarrow Wednesday. We get a couple wheelbarrows and push them around our neighborhood, collecting food for the local food pantry.

Most people are more than willing to donate—and clean out their pantries. If people answer the door and say they can't donate, we invite them to take whatever they need from our wheelbarrows.

Jay Richardson
Fort Worth, Texas

5. GREAT GIVEAWAYS

Appeal to companies' philanthropic side to help you with your outreach!

Have your kids bring in their favorite CDs, books, videos, DVDs, video games, and so on, and collect the names of distributors, publishers, or manufacturers from the labels. Then write letters to these companies, explaining your desire to use the companies' products for giveaways that will promote your church youth group to teenagers who aren't familiar with your church. Mention that you'll also accept promotional materials such as T-shirts, hats, or CD singles. (You can also mention that the giveaway will help promote their products in your community.) After you've collected a lot of items, plan a free giveaway outreach at a local high school event or at a mall or arcade. Be sure your freebies include an attached invitation to your next youth group event.

Afterward, write to the companies that sent you freebies, thanking them and telling them the success stories that those items brought to your youth group. You may even include pictures of your group and its new members!

Robert Waldrop
Rock Hill, South Carolina

6. SIDEWALK TALK

If your church is near a junior or senior high school, you can take advantage of your location as a venue for low-tech evangelism.

Our church is located on the walking route for many students on their way to a junior high school. Once a week I go out and try to get to know the students. Sometimes I give away free soft drinks, cookies, or hot chocolate. I write positive notes on the sidewalk with chalk (such as "Teenagers are cool!") or challenging questions (such as "How is God like a bubble?").

This has given me a chance to model relationship-building to students in my youth group, to encourage kids from other churches, to start conversations with students who aren't Christians, and to try to encourage better behavior (for example, not skateboarding on private property). I really enjoy building these relationships. I hope to keep it up even while the snow flies!

Ben Squires
Manitowoc, Wisconsin

7. LIVING WATER

Use bottles of water as a way to share the message of John 4:13-14.

Start a bottled water drive at your church, or raise money to purchase cases of water at a warehouse store. Have your youth group design labels that include the message of John 4:13-14. You can have each student design his or her own label, or you can use a computer graphics program to design one label for the entire youth group. Be sure the label includes the name of your church, a schedule of your Sunday services, and contact information.

Print as many copies as you have water bottles, and use clear packing tape to stick the labels on the bottles. Have the youth group hand out bottles at events or locations such as yard sales, the beach, a fair or carnival, sporting events, auctions, playgrounds, parks, or anywhere a free cold drink is welcome.

Jan Thompson
Fairview, Pennsylvania

8. AMAZING RACE OUTREACH

Adventure and challenge make this a great theme for an activity night to welcome students' friends.

Organize kids into teams of two. Set up several mini-games that are theme-based on cities or countries around the world. For instance, you might use locations and contests such as the following, giving each game a scoring system based on time limits, amount accomplished, or completing the challenge:

New York City: Bob for apples.

Mexico: Eat a hot pepper.

Iceland: Stand in a baby pool filled with ice water.

Ireland: Peel potatoes—be sure to use gloves!

Georgia: Blindfolded kids fish worms out of a tank filled with plastic peanuts and earthworms.

Throw in prizes for winners, participants, and random players. Then present the prizes at a "ceremony." We added a speaker who talked on the theme, "Who are you partnered with?"

We also included a great local band, and at the end of the evening, we all traveled to "Italy" for free pizza. As an option you can have all the mini-game locations relate to the places where your church supports missionaries.

Jason Schmock
Roseville, Minnesota

9. LOVE ONE ANOTHER

Valentine's Day is the perfect opportunity for teenagers to share God's love with others.

Before Valentine's Day, ask each teenager to open a phone book and choose the name of an individual or business to whom he or she can send a Valentine card. Instead of a normal Valentine message, encourage teenagers to share the message of God's love with the recipients. Make certain they add your church's service information and location to the cards.

On Valentine's Day, take your youth group to a local grocery store. First take a moment to pray that the recipients of your valentines will be touched by your message and seek God. Then hand out chocolates or flowers to passersby, attaching a note that includes a Scripture verse related to God's love.

Melanie Schauer
St. Louis, Missouri

10. PARKING LOT DRIVE-IN

Drive-in movies are quickly becoming a thing of the past, but they can still be a lot of fun—especially when you create your own in the church parking lot!

Simply set up a video projector and sound system in your church's parking lot on a warm evening when the facilities aren't being used for other events.

Have students bring their cars, lawn chairs, and beach blankets. Be sure they invite friends and neighborhood families. Arrange the cars around the outer limits of your "theater," and encourage everyone to sit in front of them. Project your movie on a king-size bedsheet or on a wall. Before the movie, roll in a few barbecue grills, and serve hot dogs, hamburgers, and s'mores. Make sure you unlock the building so students can use the restroom facilities.

Walter Surdacki
Campbell, California

11. BRINGING DOWN THE LIGHTS

Teenagers extend the message of Christmas into the new year with gifts, service, and prayers.

Before this activity, have your group purchase and wrap small gifts for families in your community. They could be bags of candy, small candles, or inexpensive gift certificates to a local fast food restaurant. Be sure to include your church's name on the gift tag. You may also want to include a Scripture.

In mid-January, send groups of five or six teenagers and one adult into your community in search of homes that still display outdoor Christmas lights. Each group will need an instant camera, a digital camera, or a video camera. Have teenagers give these residents the gifts, ask them to pose for pictures in front of the house, and offer to come back and help them take down the Christmas lights.

After a few hours, have groups meet back at your church to compare results. Give an award to the group that captured the most images. Afterward have everyone spend time praying together for the families they've just met. Plan for a day of service to help take down their lights.

Jacob Youmans
Orange, California

12. SEE YOU AT THE OSCARS

Draw in teenagers and their friends with this winning project—they'll be star-struck!

About three months ahead of time, we told kids that we were going to put on an Oscar night and their job was to create "movies" for the awards ceremony. We encouraged teenagers to involve their friends from school in their projects, and we asked them to submit their videos one month before the event. (It's up to you whether you want to designate themes or categories, such as drama, comedy, documentary, and so on.)

For Oscar night, we bought thick, red material and laid down a "red carpet." Kids arrived in dress-up clothes, and we showed all the videos. We recruited local youth bands to play during the ceremony, and church members acted as presenters, handing out inexpensive awards statues.

We made great connections with kids—and with schools, as some teenagers used their videos for school projects.

You can do this event with large or small groups or even conduct it as an interchurch event.

Marcel Kurtz
North Vancouver, British Columbia

13. REVERSE TRICK-OR-TREAT

Candy and costumes combine for a friendly, fun October outreach!

Have your group fill resealable plastic bags with individually wrapped candy. Also place in each bag a message with your church's information. Include an inviting thought and Scripture, such as "'For it is by grace you have been saved, through faith—and this is not from yourselves, it is the gift of God' (Ephesians 2:8)…no tricks or treats necessary!" Sometime around Halloween, have kids dress up in costumes and go door-to-door in the neighborhoods near your church. Have them ring doorbells, and when the residents answer, they can shout, "Reverse Trick-or-Treat!" and hand out bags of candy. The neighbors might be confused at first, but usually they're appreciative, and kids love to have an excuse to dress up!

Julie Riddle
Lindenwood, Illinois

14. TWELVE DAYS OF CHRISTMAS

This "reverse scavenger hunt" is a great seasonal outreach to your local community.

Every year during after-Christmas sales, we get great deals on seasonal gifts, such as candles, mini-nativity sets, and candleholders. One evening close to the 12th day of Christmas (January 5), we form teams and go on a scavenger hunt for houses that still have their Christmas lights on. (It's harder than you think!) When we find a house, we present the owners with one of the gifts we've purchased. We also give them a letter explaining the 12 days of Christmas and thanking them for celebrating with us.

We've gotten a lot of positive feedback in letters and phone calls from recipients. This outreach is well worth the minimal time and money, and our kids learn a lot!

For more information on the 12 days of Christmas, go online to the Christian Resource Institute: www.cresourcei.org/cy12days.html.

Ray Angerman
Shaliwar, Florida

15. GUYS-ONLY VIDEO GAME LOCK-IN

Video games are a common language for most guys—here's how we used video games as the basis for a great outreach.

We asked guys in our youth group to bring their PlayStation 2, Xbox, and Nintendo video game systems, along with "clean" video games, to an overnight lock-in—and we also encouraged them to bring as many friends as possible.

We set up tables and TVs around the youth room, turning it into a video game room for the night. We hooked up one system to the projector, so a game could be shown on the wall in life-size images.

Guys were invited to arrive between 8 and 10 on Friday night, but once they came inside, they had to stay until 8 a.m. We ate snacks and played video games until around midnight, when we stopped for a short Bible study and gospel presentation. Then the students went back to their video games for the rest of the night. This was a great experience for everyone—all the kids built friendships with others they'd never spent much time with before, and the unchurched kids got to hear a clear presentation of the gospel.

Leslie Linwick
Springfield, Kentucky

16. SERVING TIME

When our budget is on the plus side and we don't need to raise money for an upcoming trip or event, we charge teenagers a "service fee."

We usually start with a prayer service and a discussion about the importance Jesus placed on serving others. Then we announce the adventure, trip, fun day, or special event. We assign a required number of individual service hours to group members, hand out "service sheets," and ask kids to serve our church members or others in the community. We tell them to write short descriptions of each service experience, logging the time, and adding a reflection about how they felt. When the service sheets are due, all the teenagers share what they've learned. These trips are always more meaningful because everyone's heart is ready to receive from God.

Susan Francis
Reedsville, Ohio

17. WASHING WINDOWS, NOT FEET

When I wanted to use Jesus' foot-washing example as the basis for a community-service project, my teenagers weren't too excited about washing strangers' feet in our city's downtown area—then I prayed.

Driving through the area, I asked for an inspiration that would allow us to apply Jesus' model of servanthood. Then I noticed how dirty many of the businesses' windows looked, and the idea came to me—Jesus washed feet; we'll wash windows.

On a Saturday we formed two groups, and armed with cleaning supplies, we spent the morning washing windows. We'd also baked cookies and brownies, which we gave to the business owners when we asked permission to clean their store windows.

After we finished this project, we received many thank-you's from the community. The downtown looked great, but more importantly, we showed God's love by serving in this simple way.

Chris Horton
Portales, New Mexico

18. SOWER, SOIL, AND SEED

Use journals and "sower boards" to integrate prayer and evangelism as part of your worship service.

Purchase a few large bulletin boards, and designate them as your "sower boards." Give each teenager a small notebook, and call the notebooks your "sower journals." Read aloud Matthew 13:3-9, and on the boards make three columns titled "Sower," "Soil," and "Seed." Tell your group that a Sower is anyone who has an opportunity for outreach. Add each person's name to that column. Tell the group members that Soil denotes the people they will be trying to reach. Then tell them that Seeds are how they might share the gospel with others. Tell everyone to carry the journals with them and write down their outreach opportunities, making sure they add all the elements: the Sower, the Soil, and the Seed details of each opportunity.

Each week during your worship service, ask teenagers to transfer journal entries to the "sower boards." Spend time at the altar or sanctuary together, laying hands on names that have been added to the board and praying for those people. Continue adding boards as your list of names grows.

In the course of one year, our group ended up with 500 names of people who were presented the gospel—awesome!

Jeff McKee
Pace, Florida

19. MINI-MISSION MONDAYS

Use this idea to warm up your teenagers to the idea of mission work.

When I approached the subject of a missions trip with our youth group, the kids were initially resistant, so we chose one Monday each month to conduct a small missions project.

August: Put together back-to-school kits for needy kids

September: Raked leaves for shut-ins

October: Hosted a trick-or-treat party to raise funds for UNICEF

November: Compiled care baskets for five needy families

December: Went caroling at local nursing homes

January: Collected hats and mittens for elementary school kids

February: Delivered candy to shut-ins

March: Organized a March of Dimes fund-raiser

April: Hosted an Easter egg hunt and meal for needy kids

May: Organized a Relay for Life team

June: Hosted a fund-raiser to send a needy child to summer camp

We kept up the interest by adding fun to the activities—turning the care-basket activity into a scavenger hunt and including a fast-food progressive dinner between caroling venues.

Chris Wheeler
Bennett, Missouri

20. R.A.S. NIGHT

Help teenagers make an impact on their community with random acts of service.

We send postcards to people in our church's neighborhood one week ahead of time to let them know our youth group will be having a Random Acts of Service event. To begin the evening, teenagers gather at the church with cleaning supplies, buckets, and rags. Then we send groups of four or five young people, each with an adult leader, out into the community to ring doorbells and offer to clean whatever needs to be cleaned. (One single mom, who had a particularly bad day, had one of our groups vacuum and help with the groceries.) While many may be skeptical about a group of teenagers offering to clean without pay, most will appreciate the offer. Close your R.A.S. night by having groups go to your local shelter with sandwiches and drinks to simply offer food and a prayer.

This event is a particularly helpful way to follow up a mission trip so teenagers can "bring home" what they've learned.

Tom Stephen
Ventura, California

21. MYSTERY DINNER

(Especially good for junior highers)

Treat students and their friends to a dose of mystery-food fun with a pinch of Bible lesson!

Ask kids each to invite a friend to a special youth group dinner. Before serving dinner, give each guest a "menu" with instructions to choose items from the list (below), until they've selected four items for each of the dinner's four courses. Let kids know that they'll have to clear their plates entirely before the next course. Kids will have to guess what their mystery-course items are. Use these descriptions on your menu:

(1) Mud Slide

(2) Marble Slab

(3) Butcher's Special

(4) Eve's Temptation

(5) Hummingbird Nectar

(6) Surrender's Standard

(7) Paving Stones

(8) Chilly Shake

(9) Pick of the Meal

(10) Snake Eyes

(11) Chop Sticks

(12) Layered Delight

(13) Sam's Spade

(14) Peter's Choice

(15) Two Rivers Divide

(16) Dairyland Dice

After kids have taken a guess at their course items, serve dinner: (1) ice cream, (2) garlic bread, (3) table knife, (4) apple slices, (5) juice, (6) white napkin, (7) cookies, (8) gelatin, (9) toothpick, (10) olives, (11) carrot sticks, (12) lasagna, (13) spoon, (14) salad, (15) fork, and (16) cheese cubes.

Kids who don't have forks or knives for certain courses can improvise. Between courses, intersperse get-acquainted games or object lessons.

Rebecca Grosenbach
Colorado Springs, Colorado

22. CHRISTMAS HAYRIDE

Bundle up for festive holiday fun!

If you're able to borrow a flatbed trailer from a church member or local business owner, you can take your Christmas caroling out on the road. Fill the trailer with hay, load up your youth group, and drive through town as kids sing carols. Visit some of your community's shut-ins or elderly to share Christmas carols and home-baked holiday cookies with them. At each stop, take a photograph of the group, and send photos later to the recipients as a reminder of your visit.

When your hayride is finished, return to the church for a roaring bonfire with chili and s'mores.

Tracy Gegelin
Madison, Indiana

23. FIRST NITES

Turn Sunday nights into regular fun events that your community and your teenagers look forward to!

Designate the first Sunday night of each month as a time to connect with the community and with inactive church members. Publicize each event as "First Nite," and plan fun, non-intimidating activities that build relationships, such as roller-skating, ice-skating, bowling, going to the movies, or visiting a rock-climbing gym. Often businesses will have special rates for churches and will rent their facilities for private parties. Try to keep your costs under $10 per person for your events, so you can attract more people. If your budget allows, offer "First Timers" free attendance, or ask adult church members to sponsor them. Encourage your teenagers to offer complimentary tickets to their friends.

Your youth group will enjoy organizing, running, and attending these events. Allow kids to participate in the planning of your events to keep them fun and trendy enough to attract your community's younger crowd.

Jill Laufenberg
West Chester, Pennsylvania

24. COOKIE INVITATION

Use cookies to intrigue teenagers and entice them to your next youth group event.

Purchase a large tub of cookie dough (enough for approximately 100 cookies) at a discount warehouse store or grocery store. You might ask your youth group members to donate a dollar toward your purchase. Ask your youth group or one of your church's adult groups to make the cookies.

Have your youth group members create invitations that include one or two cookies in a bag along with a business-card-sized note that says "Want more?" on one side. On the other side of the cards, list the youth event details: name of the event, date and time, and a contact phone number and e-mail address. As youth group members hand out the cookie invitations after church or at a local teen hangout, encourage them to use the "Want more?" question to generate discussion with recipients.

This outreach activity drew 15 visitors to our youth group in just two weeks, and most of those visitors are now active members.

Michael Kirby
Powhatow, Virginia

25. CLIMB OF FAITH

Use the fast-growing sport of rock climbing to help teenagers talk about their faith.

Rent an indoor rock-climbing facility for an afternoon or evening. Publicize your event to your students and their friends, and include the facility's release form for parental approval. Make sure the facility has trained staff to monitor teenagers as they attempt an ascent up the climbing walls. Ask volunteers to come and encourage your guests in their climbing efforts, focusing on first timers.

As you wrap up your climbing time, have two or three students talk about how Christian faith is like rock climbing—it may be a struggle to get to a higher place but the experience is tremendously rewarding. Then ask students to discuss how God's Word is a foundation for their "climb of faith."

Walter Surdacki
Campbell, California

26. CELL PHONE CELEBRATION

Here's an awesome way to turn annoying cell phones into instruments of outreach.

Are you frustrated that ringing cell phones interrupt your student worship service, regardless of how many times you ask kids to turn off their phones? Turn this situation to your advantage by first asking teenagers to turn them on! If some students don't have cell phones, tell them to partner with someone who does.

Ask participants if they have programmed into their phones the number of one person who isn't attending the worship service with them. Then tell everyone to call these people and ask them to hold on for a few seconds. After everyone has connected with someone, tell the entire group to yell, "We miss you here!" Then tell participants to say goodbye, hang up, and turn off their cell phones.

Not only did we have instantaneous outreach to 130 people, but we didn't have a single cell phone ring after that!

Benny Bowman
Pell City, Alabama

27. SERVING UP KINDNESS

Serving others—literally—can create great publicity for your youth group events.

This is a great way to celebrate the last school day before spring break or Easter, or to celebrate World Kindness Day November 13.

Ask permission from a school administrator to wait tables at lunchtime in the school's cafeteria. Then contact local hardware stores to see if one would donate canvas aprons for your "waiters and waitresses." You can use fabric paint or iron-on transfers to decorate the aprons with your group's logo.

During lunch hour, have your youth group members wait tables in the school cafeteria by clearing trays, collecting trash, and cleaning off tables. They can offer to seat students and make food runs for them. At the end of the lunch hour, have the wait staff hand each "customer" a chocolate candy along with a "bill" on which is printed the details of your next youth group event.

The lunchroom staff will appreciate the extra help, and you'll tap into a wealth of potential new members!

Emily Whitehill
Barnet, Vermont

28. COMMUNITY PARTNERSHIPS

Connect with teenagers throughout your community by partnering with a local nonprofit.

For example, after our youth group helped the food bank distribute baskets to those in need, the food bank agreed to help us by sponsoring an outreach concert. School groups and other students got involved and attended because they were familiar with the food bank and its services. Also, local venues often give breaks on rental fees when you're working with a community nonprofit organization.

There are multiple benefits to this idea—our students were blessed by serving the food bank recipients, and they were able to invite unchurched friends to the concert; the food bank received help, plus food donations (through the concert's "entry fees"); and, best of all, many community teenagers heard the gospel message.

Alan Bartolome
Kahului, Hawaii

29. CHURCH MEALS ON WHEELS

Help teenagers touch the lives of needy members in your congregation.

Get a list of your congregation's shut-ins from your pastor. If you have a small congregation, work with a larger church to help serve meals to their shut-ins as well. Have your group call people on the list to tell them that members of the youth group are coming for a visit—and they're bringing lunch! Be sure to record any of your recipients' dietary restrictions.

Ask some of your students' families to make casseroles and others to make salads, placed in disposable food containers. Ask some of the teenagers to bake cookies, and have others make a fun favor to go with the meal, such as a magnet or small greeting card. Assemble meals in sectioned, covered plates, and send your group out in teams with adult volunteers. For added fun, encourage your groups to ask their recipients about local church history!

Peggy Osborne
Pittsburgh, Pennsylvania

30. COMMUNITY SNAPSHOT

Use a scavenger hunt to introduce your teenagers to servants in your community.

Before the activity, use an instant-print camera to photograph portions of objects in the community—such as half of a food-bank sign or part of a community-center building. Be sure each object is connected somehow to a person, organization, or business that serves the community so that you encourage teenagers to talk to people who serve others.

At your meeting, form teams of four or five, and give each team a photograph. Tell teams they must find the object in the photograph, and then ask a person related to that object how he or she contributes to the community. If no one associated with the object is available, teams can ask others who might be nearby how the business or organization contributes to the community. When teams return to the church, have them share their discoveries with the whole group. Then have group members pray for each community member they met and ask God to bless his or her contributions to the community.

Randy McKain and Jeff Anderson
Bemidji, Minnesota